WRITE 10K in a DAY
Accompaniment Text

AUTHOR PLANNER

Award Winning Author
LYDIA MICHAELS

SCHEDULE

AUTHOR PLANNER

Part of the Write 10K in a Day Series

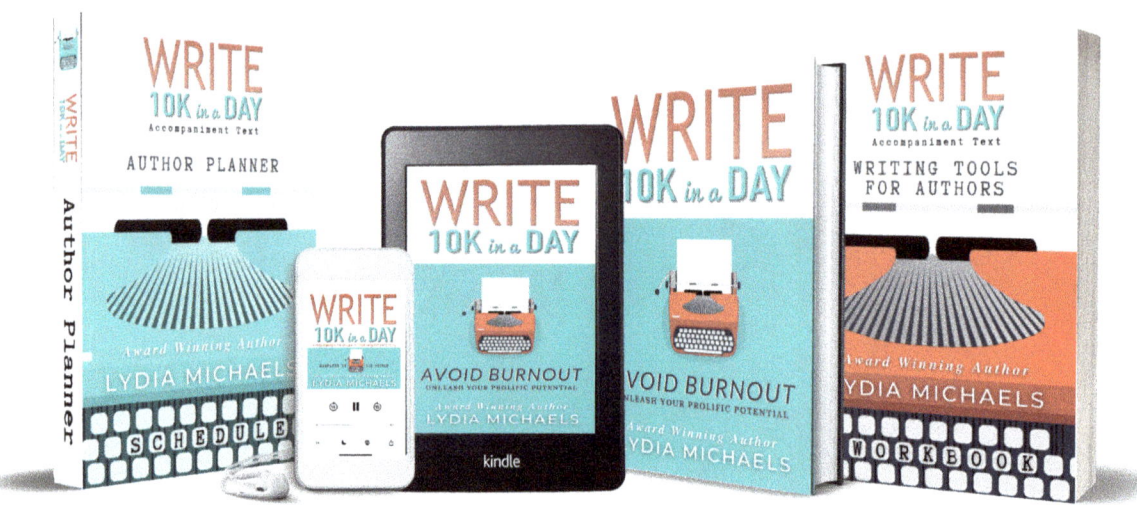

Write 10k in a Day Author Planner
Written and Produced by Lydia Michaels
www.LydiaMichaelsBooks.com
© Lydia Michaels Books 2021

Published by Bailey Brown Publishing
Cover Design by Lydia Michaels
Edited by Theresa Kohler, Oxford Comma Editing

All rights reserved.
No part of this book may be reproduced in any form or by any electronic or mechanical means, including information storage and retrieval systems, without written permission from the author, except for the use of brief quotations in a book review.

TABLE OF CONTENTS

HOW TO USE THIS PLANNER

PART ONE : A YEAR AT A GLANCE

- PUBLISHING YEAR AT A GLANCE
- MONTHLY CALENDAR
- TRAVEL ITINERARY

PART TWO : TRACKERS

- WORK IN PROGRESS (WIP) TRACKER
- SHORT-TERM GOAL TRACKER
- LONG-TERM GOAL TRACKER
- BUCKET LIST
- BIRTHDAY TRACKER
- PASSWORD LIST

PART THREE : SCHEDULE

- WEEKLY PLANNER

PART FOUR : RESOURCES

- GENERAL PUNCTUATION RULES
- CAPITALIZATION RULES
- FORMATTING NUMBERS
- FILLER WORDS & STALL WORDS
- OVERUSED WORDS
- DIALOGUE TAGS
- NOTES

HOW TO
USE THIS PLANNER

HOW TO USE THIS PLANNER

PART ONE

Part One offers an overview of the year. Use the "Publishing Year at a Glance" page to plan your release schedule, coordinate with editors, and block out needed time for book tours.

Monthly calendars follow a traditional block format and provides an extra column to assign a specific monthly focus to the many areas of your business, such as writing, editing, promo, education, and business.

Travel itineraries are provided at the end of this section to keep book tour plans organized.

PART TWO

Part Two provides various spreadsheets that help authors manage the various parts of the job. Samples are provided in the upcoming pages.

The "WIP Tracker" allows authors to shift projects at various stages of production without losing track of the individual stages of each WIP.

The "Short-Term Goal Tracker" sets incentives as rewards that remind authors to celebrate each victory, big or small. The "Long-Term Goal Tracker" focuses on broader dreams, much like a five-year plan. And the "Bucket List" works as a steady reminder that we have a life to live outside of our author existence.

The "Birthday Tracker" offers a bird's-eye view of important dates each month.

The "Password List" keeps tracks of an author's various accounts.

PART THREE

Part Three is an all-inclusive weekly planner detailed in the sample pages ahead.

PART FOUR

Part Four contains quick references for authors, such as general rules of punctuation and capitalization, a formatting guide for numbers, lists of stall phrases, filler words, and overused words to avoid, common dialogue tags, and an area for notes.

SHORT-TERM
GOAL TRACKER

"Record your goals, monitor them, and celebrate each achievement along the way. Success is not a single destination, it's the overall experience of getting there. Enjoy the journey!"

Lydia Michaels, Write 10k in a Day, 2021

SET DATE	GOAL	REWARD	DATE MET
Jan 2021	Amazon Bestseller List	Champagne w/ Friends	3/10/21
Jan 2021	Finish 4 Jasper Falls Books	Vacation	3/20/21
Jan 2021	Finish 10K Beta Edits	3 TBR Novels	2/18/21
Feb 2021	5k Followers on IG	Mani/Pedi	2/18/21
April 2021	10k Followers on IG	Celebratory Dinner!	
April 2021	Publish 40th Book	Boat Party at Sea!	

LONG-TERM GOALS

PERSONAL

Appreciate Every Day!
Live Your Best Life
#1 Objective "Be Happy"

PROFESSIONAL

New York Times Bestseller List
Wall Street Journal Bestseller List
USA Today Bestseller List

FINANCIAL

Double Income from 2020

PHYSICAL

Hit & Maintain Goal Weight
Walk Every Day
Do More Yoga

EMOTIONAL

Stop Negative Thoughts
Disassociate from Toxic People & Habits
Meditate More Often

BUCKET LIST

"You can have a life without a career, but you can't have a career without a life."

Lydia Michaels, Write 10k in a Day, 2021

Beach Picnic at Sunset

Visit Tuscany

Visit France

Pub Crawl in Ireland

Throw a Summer Party

Buy a Coastal Home

Camping Under the Stars

Learn Italian

Flash Mob

Sell a Screenplay

Pet Portugal Goats

Stare into the Pacific Ocean

Swim with the Dolphins

Moonlight Cruise

BIRTHDAY TRACKER

JAN	FEB	MAR	APR	MAY	JUNE	JULY	AUG	SEP	OCT	NOV	DEC
1	1	1	1	1	1	1	1	1	1	1	1
2	2	2	2	2	2	2	2	2	2	2	2
3 Sue	3	3	3	3	3	3	3	3	3	3	3
4	4	4	4	4	4	4	4	4 Fran	4	4	4
5	5	5	5	5 Keesha	5	5	5	5	5	5 Pop	5
6	6	6	6 Mark	6	6	6	6	6	6	6	6
7	7	7 Elle	7	7	7	7	7	7	7	7	7 Carol
8	8	8	8	8	8	8	8	8	8	8	8
9	9	9	9	9	9	9	9	9	9	9	9
10	10	10	10	10	10	10	10	10	10	10	10
11	11	11	11	11 Jen	11	11	11	11	11	11	11
12	12	12	12	12	12	12	12	12	12	12	12
13	13	13	13	13	13	13	13	13 Steve	13	13	13
14	14	14 Cassey	14	14	14	14	14	14	14	14	14
15	15	15	15	15	15 Nikki	15	15 Alishia	15	15	15	15
16	16	16	16	16	16	16	16	16	16 Mom	16	16
17	17	17	17 Mike	17	17	17	17	17 Amy	17	17	17
18	18	18	18	18	18	18	18	18	18	18	18
19	19	19	19	19	19	19	19	19	19	19	19
20	20	20	20	20	20	20	20	20	20	20	20
21	21	21	21	21	21	21	21	21	21	21	21
22	22	22 Pam	22	22	22	22	22	22	22	22	22
23	23	23	23	23	23	23	23	23 Rachel	23	23	23
24	24	24	24	24	24	24	24	24	24	24	24
25	25	25	25	25	25	25	25	25	25	25	25
26	26	26	26	26	26	26	26	26	26	26	26
27	27	27	27	27	27	27 Darron	27	27	27	27	27
28	28	28	28	28	28	28	28	28	28	28	28
29		29	29	29	29	29	29	29	29	29	29
30		30	30	30	30	30	30	30	30	30	30
31		31		31		31	31		31		31

HOW TO USE PART THREE

Enter the dates for the week.   Week of: _____

What is the most time sensitive task this week that MUST get done? That's your priority. There should only be one priority, never multiple priorities.

Priority

What task have you been putting off? That's your "frog." Handle it first thing in the morning on a selected day, before starting anything else.

Eat the Frog

Prioritize your focus for the week, selecting a *Health & Wellness* focus, a *Business* focus, and a *Craft* (writing) focus.

Health & Wellness	Business	Craft

Check off your one hour sprint each day. Make it the first thing you do.

1 HOUR SPRINT

Use task batching to group schedule. The highlighted area allows authors to "block" their schedule into two parts. Authors will be more productive if they sort creative tasks from analytic tasks. Authors desiring more structure should label tasks and goals with a specific time for a *Time Boxing* approach.

Don't forget to refuel with a healthy midday meal.   *Fuel*

Don't forget to take your vitamins or supplements.   Vitamins

Stay hydrated! Mark your water consumption throughout the day.

Take regular movement breaks and get those steps in! (10K... match that word count!)

Tally your word count at the end of each day to track progress.   Word count: ___K

Compile random tasks on the To-Do List.

Check email by the end of each day.   ☐ M ☐ T ☐ W ☐ T ☐ F

Interact on social media for 20 minutes each day.   ☐ M ☐ T ☐ W ☐ T ☐ F

Do 3 random acts of kindness by helping others each week.   *Random Acts of Kindness* ☐☐☐

Jot down any weekend obligations. Don't forget to take time for you!   *Weekend*

Delegate tasks to next week as needed.   *Next Week*

Priority: Ship Book Orders

WEEKLY PLANNER

Week of: April 4-11, 2021

Eat the Frog: Update Back Matter

WEEKLY FOCUS

Health & Wellness	Business	Craft
Massage	Goodreads Giveaway	Jasper Falls

Monday ✓
1 HOUR SPRINT ✓
- Write
- Meeting with PR
- Post Office
- Fuel ✓
- Vitamins ✓
- Word count: 10K

Tuesday ✓
1 HOUR SPRINT ✓
- Write
- Write
- Fuel ✓
- Vitamins ✓
- Word count: 10K

Wednesday ✓
1 HOUR SPRINT ✓
- Write
- Proof
- Fuel ✓
- Vitamins ✓
- Word count: 6K

Thursday
1 HOUR SPRINT
- Frog
- Giveaways
- To-Do's
- Design Book Promo
- Fuel
- Vitamins
- Word count: __K

Friday
1 HOUR SPRINT
- Schedule Next Week
- Photoshoot Friday
- Video Unboxing
- FB Live
- Fuel
- Vitamins
- Word count: __K

To-Do List
- [ ] Update Short Links
- [ ] Check Audiobook Auditions
- [ ] ARC Sign Ups
- [ ] Schedule Doc Apt
- [ ] Update FB Ads
- [ ]
- [ ]
- [ ]

Email
- [✓] M
- [✓] T
- [✓] W
- [ ] T
- [ ] F

20 Min Social
- [✓] M
- [✓] T
- [ ] W
- [ ] T
- [ ] F

Random Acts of Kindness
[✓] [✓] [ ]

Weekend
- Dinner w/ Elle & Joe Fri 8pm
- Massage Sat 10am
- Liz's B-day Sat 7pm

Next Week
- Jasper Falls Deadline
- Beta Notes Due
- Vamp Series Sale

OVERFLOW

On the left of each weekly planner is a page for OVERFLOW. This workspace will help authors become more efficient by recording unexpected setbacks, distractions, and tracking reminders. It focuses on maintaining a positive mindset to keep authors moving in a forward motion by offering a space to record a high point, note gratitude, identify areas for improvement, and write a weekly affirmation.

SAMPLE

Samples have been provided on the next two pages.

TASK BATCHING

Task Batching groups similar activities in a way that increases focus and productivity and diminish multitasking. Rather that switch tasks frequently, try working in blocks of time. This will avoid time loss from wasted time.

PASSIVE ACTIVITIES

Passive Activities are activities that require minimal focus and can often be grouped. An example of grouping passive activities might be taking a walk while returning a phone call. By grouping passive activities, especially during an afternoon lag, the brain gets a break and can redirect your energy. Never group activities that require various forms of focus.

WRITE 10K IN A DAY

To better understand strategies such as *Time Boxing* and *Time Blocking*, as well as other proficient methods used to increase productivity, please check out the *Write 10K in a Day* book where those and more great tips are taught.

For other time saving author tools, you may also like the *Write 10K in a Day Workbook*. For additional tips and tricks, be sure to follow @Lydia_Michaels_Books and the Write 10K in a Day Instagram page @Write10KinaDay.

OVERFLOW

NOTES: M T W T F S S

Back Matter Updated on:
- KDP ✓
- GP ✓
- D2D ✓
- Kobo ✓
- Apple ✓

Proof pg. 203 - 205

Make word bank for hero

Call Theresa on Walk!

THIS WEEK'S AFFIRMATION:

"Silence is the death of opportunity."

This week I will practice being more direct and vocal about my needs.

THIS WEEK'S HIGH POINT:

5 star review from bookstagrammer

I'M GRATEFUL FOR:

The beautiful weather lately

THIS WEEK'S DISTRACTION:

Relatives popping in unannounced

HOW CAN I IMPROVE?

Be more direct: "I'm very busy. Can I call you after work today?" Do not engage or you will encourage more pop in visits during work hours.

REMINDERS:

Email about author signing
Order new book marks
Send flowers to Liz

GET THE FULL EXPERIENCE

The **Write 10K in a Day Author Planner** is part of the *Write 10K in a Day* series which includes Lydia Michaels' groundbreaking author guide, ***Write 10K in a Day: Avoid Burnout and Unleash Your Prolific Potential*** (available in print, digital, and **audiobook**), and the ***Write 10K in a Day Workbook***.

The *Write 10K in a Day* text takes a comprehensive look at business essentials such as the publishing process, managing social media, finding a healthy balance between life and time on the job, and achieving sustainable success in the book industry. Michaels shares years of experience in a warm and personal manner that grips the reader, inspires, and even gets a few laughs.

For educational videos, author resources, and ongoing inspiration, follow Lydia Michaels and the *Write 10K in a Day* series on Instagram **@Write10KinaDay** and **@Lydia_Michaels_Books**.

Do you have suggestions to improve this planner or other books in the Write 10K in a Day series?

Email Lydia Michaels at Lydia@LydiaMichaelsBooks.com.

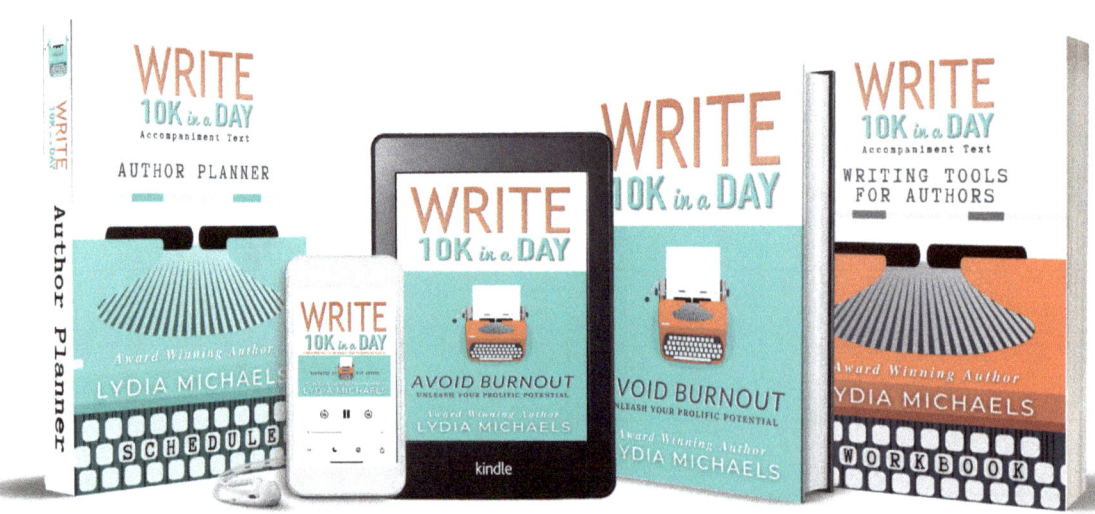

PART I
A YEAR AT A GLANCE

NOTES

Jan Feb Mar Apr May Jun Jul Aug Sep Oct Nov Dec

PUBLISHING
YEAR AT GLANCE

Jan	Feb	Mar
Apr	May	Jun
Jul	Aug	Sep
Oct	Nov	Dec

Research Write Edit Release Promote Events Learn Vacation

MONTH:

SUNDAY	MONDAY	TUESDAY	WEDNESDA

"Stop apologizing for taking time to meet your needs."

Lydia Michaels, Write 10K in a Day, 2021

THURSDAY	FRIDAY	SATURDAY	FOCUS
			WRITING:
			EDITING:
			PROMO:
			EDUCATION:
			BUSINESS:

MONTH:

SUNDAY	MONDAY	TUESDAY	WEDNESDA

taking care of you, mentally, physically, and spiritually is the first step in your journey to success."

Lydia Michaels, Write 10K in a Day, 2021

WRITE 10K in a DAY

THURSDAY	FRIDAY	SATURDAY	FOCUS
			WRITING:
			EDITING:
			PROMO:
			EDUCATION:
			BUSINESS:

MONTH:

SUNDAY	MONDAY	TUESDAY	WEDNESDAY

"Establishing boundaries is a strength, not a weakness."

Lydia Michaels, Write 10K in a Day, 2021

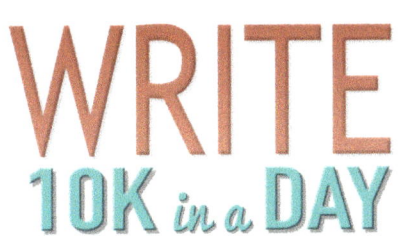

THURSDAY	FRIDAY	SATURDAY	FOCUS
			WRITING:
			EDITING:
			PROMO:
			EDUCATION:
			BUSINESS:

MONTH:

SUNDAY	MONDAY	TUESDAY	WEDNESDA

"Quitting what isn't working can often turn into a win if you're able to redirect your journey without wasting time on guilt, shame, or blame."

Lydia Michaels, Write 10K in a Day, 2021

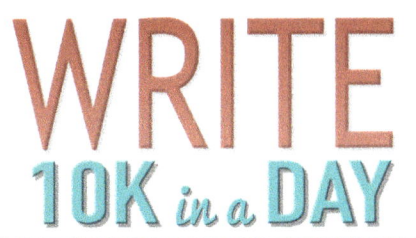

THURSDAY	FRIDAY	SATURDAY	FOCUS
			WRITING:
			EDITING:
			PROMO:
			EDUCATION:
			BUSINESS:

MONTH:

SUNDAY	MONDAY	TUESDAY	WEDNESDA

"While success is relative, other people's success is completely irrelevant to yours."

Lydia Michaels, Write 10K in a Day, 2021

WRITE 10K in a DAY

THURSDAY	FRIDAY	SATURDAY	FOCUS
			WRITING:
			EDITING:
			PROMO:
			EDUCATION:
			BUSINESS:

MONTH:

SUNDAY	MONDAY	TUESDAY	WEDNESDAY

Positivity manifests positive outcomes. Negativity attracts failure and toxicity."

Lydia Michaels, Write 10K in a Day, 2021

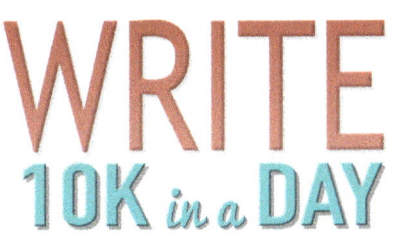

THURSDAY	FRIDAY	SATURDAY	FOCUS
			WRITING:
			EDITING:
			PROMO:
			EDUCATION:
			BUSINESS:

MONTH:

SUNDAY	MONDAY	TUESDAY	WEDNESDA

"The less you live the less alive you will be."

Lydia Michaels, Write 10K in a Day, 2021

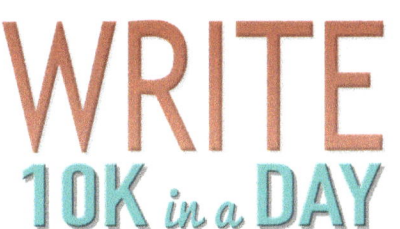

THURSDAY	FRIDAY	SATURDAY	FOCUS
			WRITING:
			EDITING:
			PROMO:
			EDUCATION:
			BUSINESS:

MONTH:

SUNDAY	MONDAY	TUESDAY	WEDNESDA

Don't let your limits discourage you. Every step, no matter how big or small, will get you closer to your goals."

Lydia Michaels, Write 10K in a Day, 2021

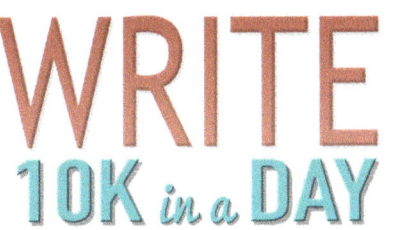

THURSDAY	FRIDAY	SATURDAY	FOCUS
			WRITING:
			EDITING:
			PROMO:
			EDUCATION:
			BUSINESS:

MONTH:

SUNDAY	MONDAY	TUESDAY	WEDNESDA

ou are your first and best advocate. If you don't establish
undaries, you can't expect others to respect them."

Lydia Michaels, Write 10K in a Day, 2021

WRITE 10K in a DAY

THURSDAY	FRIDAY	SATURDAY	FOCUS
			WRITING:
			EDITING:
			PROMO:
			EDUCATION:
			BUSINESS:

MONTH:

SUNDAY	MONDAY	TUESDAY	WEDNESDAY

Quality work begins with taking quality care of the creator."

Lydia Michaels, Write 10K in a Day, 2021

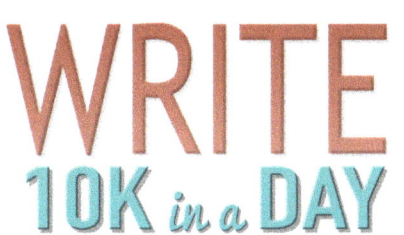

THURSDAY	FRIDAY	SATURDAY	FOCUS
			WRITING:
			EDITING:
			PROMO:
			EDUCATION:
			BUSINESS:

MONTH:

SUNDAY	MONDAY	TUESDAY	WEDNESDAY

"We're all navigating some level of a shit show..."

Lydia Michaels, Write 10K in a Day, 2021

THURSDAY	FRIDAY	SATURDAY	FOCUS
			WRITING:
			EDITING:
			PROMO:
			EDUCATION:
			BUSINESS:

MONTH:

SUNDAY	MONDAY	TUESDAY	WEDNESDAY

"You've put in your time and worked hard to get where you are. Nothing about your position is by chance. Everything about your trajectory is strategized."

　　　　　　　　Lydia Michaels, Write 10K in a Day, 2021

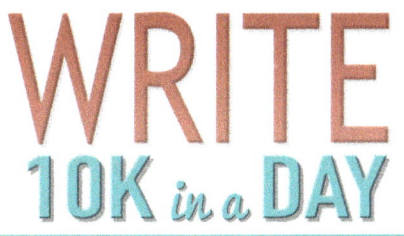

THURSDAY	FRIDAY	SATURDAY	FOCUS
			WRITING:
			EDITING:
			PROMO:
			EDUCATION:
			BUSINESS:

TRAVEL
ITINERARY

DESTINATION:

DURATION OF STAY:

FLIGHT DEPARTURE:

RETURNING FLIGHT DEPARTURE:

HOTEL DETAILS:

FLIGHT ARRIVAL:

RETURNING FLIGHT ARRIVAL:

DAY 1
- AUTHOR EVENTS:
- NETWORKING:

DAY 2
- AUTHOR EVENTS:
- NETWORKING:

DAY 3
- AUTHOR EVENTS:
- NETWORKING:

DAY 4
- AUTHOR EVENTS:
- NETWORKING:

TRAVEL ITINERARY

DESTINATION:	DURATION OF STAY:

FLIGHT DEPARTURE:

    RETURNING FLIGHT DEPARTURE:

HOTEL DETAILS:

FLIGHT ARRIVAL:

    RETURNING FLIGHT ARRIVAL:

	AUTHOR EVENTS:	NETWORKING:
DAY 1		
DAY 2	AUTHOR EVENTS:	NETWORKING:
DAY 3	AUTHOR EVENTS:	NETWORKING:
DAY 4	AUTHOR EVENTS:	NETWORKING:

TRAVEL
ITINERARY

| DESTINATION: | DURATION OF STAY: |

FLIGHT DEPARTURE:

    RETURNING FLIGHT DEPARTURE:

HOTEL DETAILS:

FLIGHT ARRIVAL:

    RETURNING FLIGHT ARRIVAL:

DAY 1 — AUTHOR EVENTS: — NETWORKING:

DAY 2 — AUTHOR EVENTS: — NETWORKING:

DAY 3 — AUTHOR EVENTS: — NETWORKING:

DAY 4 — AUTHOR EVENTS: — NETWORKING:

TRAVEL
ITINERARY

DESTINATION:

DURATION OF STAY:

FLIGHT DEPARTURE:

RETURNING FLIGHT DEPARTURE:

HOTEL DETAILS:

FLIGHT ARRIVAL:

RETURNING FLIGHT ARRIVAL:

DAY 1 | **AUTHOR EVENTS:** | **NETWORKING:**

DAY 2 | **AUTHOR EVENTS:** | **NETWORKING:**

DAY 3 | **AUTHOR EVENTS:** | **NETWORKING:**

DAY 4 | **AUTHOR EVENTS:** | **NETWORKING:**

TRAVEL ITINERARY

DESTINATION:

DURATION OF STAY:

FLIGHT DEPARTURE:

RETURNING FLIGHT DEPARTURE:

HOTEL DETAILS:

FLIGHT ARRIVAL:

RETURNING FLIGHT ARRIVAL:

DAY 1
- AUTHOR EVENTS:
- NETWORKING:

DAY 2
- AUTHOR EVENTS:
- NETWORKING:

DAY 3
- AUTHOR EVENTS:
- NETWORKING:

DAY 4
- AUTHOR EVENTS:
- NETWORKING:

W.I.P. TRACKER

BOOK TITLE

- WRITING
- PROOFING
- EDITOR (1-3 ROUNDS)
- REVISIONS
- PROOFREADER
- BETAS
- COVER DESIGN*
- OPEN PREORDERS*
- POST ON GOODREADS*
- SCHEDULE PROMO
- AUDIOBOOK*
- FORMATTING
- FINAL READ
- PITCH OR UPLOAD MS
- RELEASED!

*Dependent on if an author intends to publish title independently or traditionally

SHORT-TERM
GOAL TRACKER

"Record your goals, monitor them, and celebrate each achievement along the way. Success is not a single destination, it's the overall experience of getting there. Enjoy the journey!"

Lydia Michaels, Write 10k in a Day, 2021

SET DATE	GOAL	REWARD	DATE MET

LONG-TERM GOALS

PERSONAL

PROFESSIONAL

FINANCIAL

PHYSICAL

EMOTIONAL

BUCKET LIST

"You can have a life without a career, but you can't have a career without a life."

Lydia Michaels, Write 10k in a Day, 2021

BIRTHDAY TRACKER

JAN	FEB	MAR	APR	MAY	JUNE	JULY	AUG	SEP	OCT	NOV	DEC
1	1	1	1	1	1	1	1	1	1	1	1
2	2	2	2	2	2	2	2	2	2	2	2
3	3	3	3	3	3	3	3	3	3	3	3
4	4	4	4	4	4	4	4	4	4	4	4
5	5	5	5	5	5	5	5	5	5	5	5
6	6	6	6	6	6	6	6	6	6	6	6
7	7	7	7	7	7	7	7	7	7	7	7
8	8	8	8	8	8	8	8	8	8	8	8
9	9	9	9	9	9	9	9	9	9	9	9
10	10	10	10	10	10	10	10	10	10	10	10
11	11	11	11	11	11	11	11	11	11	11	11
12	12	12	12	12	12	12	12	12	12	12	12
13	13	13	13	13	13	13	13	13	13	13	13
14	14	14	14	14	14	14	14	14	14	14	14
15	15	15	15	15	15	15	15	15	15	15	15
16	16	16	16	16	16	16	16	16	16	16	16
17	17	17	17	17	17	17	17	17	17	17	17
18	18	18	18	18	18	18	18	18	18	18	18
19	19	19	19	19	19	19	19	19	19	19	19
20	20	20	20	20	20	20	20	20	20	20	20
21	21	21	21	21	21	21	21	21	21	21	21
22	22	22	22	22	22	22	22	22	22	22	22
23	23	23	23	23	23	23	23	23	23	23	23
24	24	24	24	24	24	24	24	24	24	24	24
25	25	25	25	25	25	25	25	25	25	25	25
26	26	26	26	26	26	26	26	26	26	26	26
27	27	27	27	27	27	27	27	27	27	27	27
28	28	28	28	28	28	28	28	28	28	28	28
29		29	29	29	29	29	29	29	29	29	29
30		30	30	30	30	30	30	30	30	30	30
31		31		31		31	31		31		31

PASSWORD LIST

ACCOUNT   PASSWORD

PART III
SCHEDULE

OVERFLOW

NOTES: M T W T F S S

THIS WEEK'S AFFIRMATION:

THIS WEEK'S HIGH POINT:

I'M GRATEFUL FOR:

THIS WEEK'S DISTRACTION:

HOW CAN I IMPROVE?

REMINDERS:

Priority

WEEKLY PLANNER

Eat the Frog

Week of: _____

WEEKLY FOCUS

Health & Wellness | Business | Craft

Monday
1 HOUR SPRINT

Fuel
Vitamins

Word count: ___K

Tuesday
1 HOUR SPRINT

Fuel
Vitamins

Word count: ___K

Wednesday
1 HOUR SPRINT

Fuel
Vitamins

Word count: ___K

Thursday
1 HOUR SPRINT

Fuel
Vitamins

Word count: ___K

Friday
1 HOUR SPRINT

Fuel
Vitamins

Word count: ___K

To-Do List | Email | 20 Min Social | Weekend | Next Week

☐ M M ☐
☐ T T ☐
☐ W W ☐
☐ T T ☐
☐ F F ☐

Random Acts of Kindness

☐ ☐ ☐

OVERFLOW

NOTES: M T W T F S S

THIS WEEK'S AFFIRMATION:

THIS WEEK'S HIGH POINT:

I'M GRATEFUL FOR:

THIS WEEK'S DISTRACTION:

HOW CAN I IMPROVE?

REMINDERS:

Priority

WEEKLY PLANNER

Eat the Frog

Week of: _____

WEEKLY FOCUS

Health & Wellness	Business	Craft

Monday
1 HOUR SPRINT

Fuel
Vitamins

Word count: ___K

Tuesday
1 HOUR SPRINT

Fuel
Vitamins

Word count: ___K

Wednesday
1 HOUR SPRINT

Fuel
Vitamins

Word count: ___K

Thursday
1 HOUR SPRINT

Fuel
Vitamins

Word count: ___K

Friday
1 HOUR SPRINT

Fuel
Vitamins

Word count: ___K

To-Do List

- ☐ _____
- ☐ _____
- ☐ _____
- ☐ _____
- ☐ _____
- ☐ _____
- ☐ _____
- ☐ _____

Email
- ☐ M
- ☐ T
- ☐ W
- ☐ T
- ☐ F

20 Min Social
- M ☐
- T ☐
- W ☐
- T ☐
- F ☐

Random Acts of Kindness
☐ ☐ ☐

Weekend

Next Week

OVERFLOW

NOTES: M T W T F S S

THIS WEEK'S AFFIRMATION:

THIS WEEK'S HIGH POINT:

I'M GRATEFUL FOR:

THIS WEEK'S DISTRACTION:

HOW CAN I IMPROVE?

REMINDERS:

Priority

WEEKLY PLANNER

Eat the Frog

Week of: _____

WEEKLY FOCUS

Health & Wellness	Business	Craft

Monday
1 HOUR SPRINT

Fuel
Vitamins

Word count: ___K

Tuesday
1 HOUR SPRINT

Fuel
Vitamins

Word count: ___K

Wednesday
1 HOUR SPRINT

Fuel
Vitamins

Word count: ___K

Thursday
1 HOUR SPRINT

Fuel
Vitamins

Word count: ___K

Friday
1 HOUR SPRINT

Fuel
Vitamins

Word count: ___K

To-Do List
- ☐ _____
- ☐ _____
- ☐ _____
- ☐ _____
- ☐ _____
- ☐ _____
- ☐ _____
- ☐ _____

Email
- ☐ M
- ☐ T
- ☐ W
- ☐ T
- ☐ F

20 Min Social
- M ☐
- T ☐
- W ☐
- T ☐
- F ☐

Random Acts of Kindness
☐ ☐ ☐

Weekend

Next Week

OVERFLOW

NOTES: M T W T F S S

THIS WEEK'S AFFIRMATION:

THIS WEEK'S HIGH POINT: | **I'M GRATEFUL FOR:**

THIS WEEK'S DISTRACTION: | **HOW CAN I IMPROVE?**

REMINDERS:

Priority

WEEKLY PLANNER

Eat the Frog

Week of: _____

WEEKLY FOCUS

Health & Wellness	Business	Craft

Monday	Tuesday	Wednesday	Thursday	Friday
1 HOUR SPRINT	1 HOUR SPRINT	1 HOUR SPRINT	1 HOUR SPRINT	1 HOUR SPRINT

Fuel / Vitamins (each day)

Word count: ___K (each day)

To-Do List
- ☐ _____
- ☐ _____
- ☐ _____
- ☐ _____
- ☐ _____
- ☐ _____
- ☐ _____
- ☐ _____

Email
☐ M
☐ T
☐ W
☐ T
☐ F

20 Min Social
M ☐
T ☐
W ☐
T ☐
F ☐

Random Acts of Kindness
☐ ☐ ☐

Weekend

Next Week

OVERFLOW

NOTES: M T W T F S S

THIS WEEK'S AFFIRMATION:

THIS WEEK'S HIGH POINT:

I'M GRATEFUL FOR:

THIS WEEK'S DISTRACTION:

HOW CAN I IMPROVE?

REMINDERS:

Priority

WEEKLY PLANNER

Eat the Frog

Week of: _____

WEEKLY FOCUS

Health & Wellness	Business	Craft

Monday
1 HOUR SPRINT

Fuel
Vitamins

Word count: ___K

Tuesday
1 HOUR SPRINT

Fuel
Vitamins

Word count: ___K

Wednesday
1 HOUR SPRINT

Fuel
Vitamins

Word count: ___K

Thursday
1 HOUR SPRINT

Fuel
Vitamins

Word count: ___K

Friday
1 HOUR SPRINT

Fuel
Vitamins

Word count: ___K

To-Do List
- ☐ _____
- ☐ _____
- ☐ _____
- ☐ _____
- ☐ _____
- ☐ _____
- ☐ _____
- ☐ _____

Email
- ☐ M
- ☐ T
- ☐ W
- ☐ T
- ☐ F

20 Min Social
- M ☐
- T ☐
- W ☐
- T ☐
- F ☐

Random Acts of Kindness
☐ ☐ ☐

Weekend

Next Week

OVERFLOW

NOTES: M T W T F S S

THIS WEEK'S AFFIRMATION:

THIS WEEK'S HIGH POINT:

I'M GRATEFUL FOR:

THIS WEEK'S DISTRACTION:

HOW CAN I IMPROVE?

REMINDERS:

Priority

WEEKLY PLANNER

Eat the Frog

Week of: _____

WEEKLY FOCUS

Health & Wellness	Business	Craft

Monday
1 HOUR SPRINT

Fuel
Vitamins

Word count: ___K

Tuesday
1 HOUR SPRINT

Fuel
Vitamins

Word count: ___K

Wednesday
1 HOUR SPRINT

Fuel
Vitamins

Word count: ___K

Thursday
1 HOUR SPRINT

Fuel
Vitamins

Word count: ___K

Friday
1 HOUR SPRINT

Fuel
Vitamins

Word count: ___K

To-Do List
☐ _____
☐ _____
☐ _____
☐ _____
☐ _____
☐ _____
☐ _____

Email
☐ M
☐ T
☐ W
☐ T
☐ F

20 Min Social
M ☐
T ☐
W ☐
T ☐
F ☐

Weekend

Next Week

Random Acts of Kindness
☐ ☐ ☐

OVERFLOW

NOTES: M T W T F S S

THIS WEEK'S AFFIRMATION:

THIS WEEK'S HIGH POINT:

I'M GRATEFUL FOR:

THIS WEEK'S DISTRACTION:

HOW CAN I IMPROVE?

REMINDERS:

Priority | # WEEKLY PLANNER | Eat the Frog

Week of: _____

WEEKLY FOCUS

Health & Wellness	Business	Craft

Monday | Tuesday | Wednesday | Thursday | Friday

1 HOUR SPRINT | 1 HOUR SPRINT | 1 HOUR SPRINT | 1 HOUR SPRINT | 1 HOUR SPRINT

Fuel Vitamins (×5)

Word count: ___K (×5)

To-Do List

- [ ] _____
- [ ] _____
- [ ] _____
- [ ] _____
- [ ] _____
- [ ] _____
- [ ] _____
- [ ] _____

Email

- [ ] M
- [ ] T
- [ ] W
- [ ] T
- [ ] F

20 Min Social

- M [ ]
- T [ ]
- W [ ]
- T [ ]
- F [ ]

Random Acts of Kindness

[ ] [ ] [ ]

Weekend

Next Week

OVERFLOW

NOTES: M T W T F S S

THIS WEEK'S AFFIRMATION:

THIS WEEK'S HIGH POINT:

I'M GRATEFUL FOR:

THIS WEEK'S DISTRACTION:

HOW CAN I IMPROVE?

REMINDERS:

Priority

WEEKLY PLANNER

Eat the Frog

Week of: _____

WEEKLY FOCUS

Health & Wellness	Business	Craft

Monday
1 HOUR SPRINT

Fuel Vitamins

Word count: ___K

Tuesday
1 HOUR SPRINT

Fuel Vitamins

Word count: ___K

Wednesday
1 HOUR SPRINT

Fuel Vitamins

Word count: ___K

Thursday
1 HOUR SPRINT

Fuel Vitamins

Word count: ___K

Friday
1 HOUR SPRINT

Fuel Vitamins

Word count: ___K

To-Do List
☐ _____
☐ _____
☐ _____
☐ _____
☐ _____
☐ _____
☐ _____
☐ _____

Email
☐ M
☐ T
☐ W
☐ T
☐ F

20 Min Social
M ☐
T ☐
W ☐
T ☐
F ☐

Random Acts of Kindness
☐ ☐ ☐

Weekend

Next Week

OVERFLOW

NOTES: M T W T F S S

THIS WEEK'S AFFIRMATION:

THIS WEEK'S HIGH POINT:

I'M GRATEFUL FOR:

THIS WEEK'S DISTRACTION:

HOW CAN I IMPROVE?

REMINDERS:

Priority

WEEKLY PLANNER

Eat the Frog

Week of: _____

WEEKLY FOCUS

Health & Wellness	Business	Craft

Monday
1 HOUR SPRINT

Fuel Vitamins

Word count: ___K

Tuesday
1 HOUR SPRINT

Fuel Vitamins

Word count: ___K

Wednesday
1 HOUR SPRINT

Fuel Vitamins

Word count: ___K

Thursday
1 HOUR SPRINT

Fuel Vitamins

Word count: ___K

Friday
1 HOUR SPRINT

Fuel Vitamins

Word count: ___K

To-Do List

Email

20 Min Social

☐ M   M ☐
☐ T   T ☐
☐ W   W ☐
☐ T   T ☐
☐ F   F ☐

Weekend

Next Week

Random Acts of Kindness

☐ ☐ ☐

OVERFLOW

NOTES: M T W T F S S

THIS WEEK'S AFFIRMATION:

THIS WEEK'S HIGH POINT:

I'M GRATEFUL FOR:

THIS WEEK'S DISTRACTION:

HOW CAN I IMPROVE?

REMINDERS:

Priority

WEEKLY PLANNER

Eat the Frog

Week of: _____

WEEKLY FOCUS

Health & Wellness | Business | Craft

Monday
1 HOUR SPRINT

Fuel
Vitamins

Word count:___K

Tuesday
1 HOUR SPRINT

Fuel
Vitamins

Word count:___K

Wednesday
1 HOUR SPRINT

Fuel
Vitamins

Word count:___K

Thursday
1 HOUR SPRINT

Fuel
Vitamins

Word count:___K

Friday
1 HOUR SPRINT

Fuel
Vitamins

Word count:___K

To-Do List

Email

20 Min Social

☐ M   M ☐
☐ T   T ☐
☐ W   W ☐
☐ T   T ☐
☐ F   F ☐

Weekend

Next Week

Random Acts of Kindness

☐ ☐ ☐

OVERFLOW

NOTES: M T W T F S S

THIS WEEK'S AFFIRMATION:

THIS WEEK'S HIGH POINT:

I'M GRATEFUL FOR:

THIS WEEK'S DISTRACTION:

HOW CAN I IMPROVE?

REMINDERS:

Priority

WEEKLY PLANNER

Eat the Frog

Week of: _____

WEEKLY FOCUS

Health & Wellness	Business	Craft

Monday
1 HOUR SPRINT

Fuel
Vitamins

Word count: ___K

Tuesday
1 HOUR SPRINT

Fuel
Vitamins

Word count: ___K

Wednesday
1 HOUR SPRINT

Fuel
Vitamins

Word count: ___K

Thursday
1 HOUR SPRINT

Fuel
Vitamins

Word count: ___K

Friday
1 HOUR SPRINT

Fuel
Vitamins

Word count: ___K

To-Do List
☐ _____
☐ _____
☐ _____
☐ _____
☐ _____
☐ _____
☐ _____
☐ _____

Email
☐ M
☐ T
☐ W
☐ T
☐ F

20 Min Social
M ☐
T ☐
W ☐
T ☐
F ☐

Random Acts of Kindness
☐ ☐ ☐

Weekend

Next Week

OVERFLOW

NOTES: M T W T F S S

THIS WEEK'S AFFIRMATION:

THIS WEEK'S HIGH POINT:

I'M GRATEFUL FOR:

THIS WEEK'S DISTRACTION:

HOW CAN I IMPROVE?

REMINDERS:

Priority | **WEEKLY PLANNER** | Eat the Frog

Week of: _____

WEEKLY FOCUS

Health & Wellness	Business	Craft

Monday | Tuesday | Wednesday | Thursday | Friday

1 HOUR SPRINT | 1 HOUR SPRINT | 1 HOUR SPRINT | 1 HOUR SPRINT | 1 HOUR SPRINT

Fuel / Vitamins (each day)

Word count: ___K (each day)

To-Do List

☐ _____
☐ _____
☐ _____
☐ _____
☐ _____
☐ _____
☐ _____
☐ _____

Email
☐ M
☐ T
☐ W
☐ T
☐ F

20 Min Social
M ☐
T ☐
W ☐
T ☐
F ☐

Random Acts of Kindness
☐ ☐ ☐

Weekend

Next Week

OVERFLOW

NOTES: M T W T F S S

THIS WEEK'S AFFIRMATION:

THIS WEEK'S HIGH POINT:

I'M GRATEFUL FOR:

THIS WEEK'S DISTRACTION:

HOW CAN I IMPROVE?

REMINDERS:

Priority

WEEKLY PLANNER

Eat the Frog

Week of: _____

WEEKLY FOCUS

Health & Wellness	Business	Craft

Monday	Tuesday	Wednesday	Thursday	Friday
1 HOUR SPRINT	1 HOUR SPRINT	1 HOUR SPRINT	1 HOUR SPRINT	1 HOUR SPRINT
Fuel / Vitamins	Fuel / Vitamins	Fuel / Vitamins	Fuel / Vitamins	Fuel / Vitamins
Word count: ___K	Word count: ___K	Word count: ___K	Word count: ___K	Word count: ___K

To-Do List · Email · 20 Min Social · Weekend · Next Week

- ☐ _____
- ☐ _____
- ☐ _____
- ☐ _____
- ☐ _____
- ☐ _____
- ☐ _____
- ☐ _____

Email: ☐ M ☐ T ☐ W ☐ T ☐ F

20 Min Social: ☐ M ☐ T ☐ W ☐ T ☐ F

Random Acts of Kindness ☐ ☐ ☐

OVERFLOW

NOTES: M T W T F S S

THIS WEEK'S AFFIRMATION:

THIS WEEK'S HIGH POINT:

I'M GRATEFUL FOR:

THIS WEEK'S DISTRACTION:

HOW CAN I IMPROVE?

REMINDERS:

Priority | # WEEKLY PLANNER | Eat the Frog

Week of: _____

WEEKLY FOCUS

Health & Wellness	Business	Craft

Monday | Tuesday | Wednesday | Thursday | Friday

1 HOUR SPRINT | 1 HOUR SPRINT | 1 HOUR SPRINT | 1 HOUR SPRINT | 1 HOUR SPRINT

Fuel / Vitamins (each day)

Word count: ___K | Word count: ___K | Word count: ___K | Word count: ___K | Word count: ___K

To-Do List | Email | 20 Min Social | Weekend | Next Week

- ☐ _____
- ☐ _____
- ☐ _____
- ☐ _____
- ☐ _____
- ☐ _____
- ☐ _____
- ☐ _____

Email / 20 Min Social:
- ☐ M M ☐
- ☐ T T ☐
- ☐ W W ☐
- ☐ T T ☐
- ☐ F F ☐

Random Acts of Kindness
☐ ☐ ☐

OVERFLOW

NOTES: M T W T F S S

THIS WEEK'S AFFIRMATION:

THIS WEEK'S HIGH POINT:

I'M GRATEFUL FOR:

THIS WEEK'S DISTRACTION:

HOW CAN I IMPROVE?

REMINDERS:

Priority

WEEKLY PLANNER

Eat the Frog

Week of: _____

WEEKLY FOCUS

Health & Wellness	Business	Craft

Monday
1 HOUR SPRINT

Fuel Vitamins

Word count:___K

Tuesday
1 HOUR SPRINT

Fuel Vitamins

Word count:___K

Wednesday
1 HOUR SPRINT

Fuel Vitamins

Word count:___K

Thursday
1 HOUR SPRINT

Fuel Vitamins

Word count:___K

Friday
1 HOUR SPRINT

Fuel Vitamins

Word count:___K

To-Do List
- ☐ _____
- ☐ _____
- ☐ _____
- ☐ _____
- ☐ _____
- ☐ _____
- ☐ _____
- ☐ _____

Email / 20 Min Social
- ☐ M M ☐
- ☐ T T ☐
- ☐ W W ☐
- ☐ T T ☐
- ☐ F F ☐

Random Acts of Kindness
☐ ☐ ☐

Weekend

Next Week

OVERFLOW

NOTES: M T W T F S S

THIS WEEK'S AFFIRMATION:

THIS WEEK'S HIGH POINT:	I'M GRATEFUL FOR:
THIS WEEK'S DISTRACTION:	HOW CAN I IMPROVE?

REMINDERS:

Priority | # WEEKLY PLANNER | Eat the Frog

Week of: _____

WEEKLY FOCUS

Health & Wellness	Business	Craft

Monday	Tuesday	Wednesday	Thursday	Friday
1 HOUR SPRINT	1 HOUR SPRINT	1 HOUR SPRINT	1 HOUR SPRINT	1 HOUR SPRINT
Fuel / Vitamins	Fuel / Vitamins	Fuel / Vitamins	Fuel / Vitamins	Fuel / Vitamins
Word count:___K	Word count:___K	Word count:___K	Word count:___K	Word count:___K

To-Do List
- _____
- _____
- _____
- _____
- _____
- _____
- _____
- _____

Email
- ☐ M
- ☐ T
- ☐ W
- ☐ T
- ☐ F

20 Min Social
- M ☐
- T ☐
- W ☐
- T ☐
- F ☐

Random Acts of Kindness
☐ ☐ ☐

Weekend

Next Week

OVERFLOW

NOTES: M T W T F S S

THIS WEEK'S AFFIRMATION:

THIS WEEK'S HIGH POINT:

I'M GRATEFUL FOR:

THIS WEEK'S DISTRACTION:

HOW CAN I IMPROVE?

REMINDERS:

Priority

WEEKLY PLANNER

Eat the Frog

Week of: _____

WEEKLY FOCUS

Health & Wellness	Business	Craft

Monday	Tuesday	Wednesday	Thursday	Friday
1 HOUR SPRINT	1 HOUR SPRINT	1 HOUR SPRINT	1 HOUR SPRINT	1 HOUR SPRINT

Fuel / Vitamins (each day)

Word count: ___K Word count: ___K Word count: ___K Word count: ___K Word count: ___K

To-Do List   Email   20 Min Social   Weekend   Next Week

- ☐ _____
- ☐ _____
- ☐ _____
- ☐ _____
- ☐ _____
- ☐ _____
- ☐ _____
- ☐ _____

Email / 20 Min Social:
- ☐ M M ☐
- ☐ T T ☐
- ☐ W W ☐
- ☐ T T ☐
- ☐ F F ☐

Random Acts of Kindness
☐ ☐ ☐

OVERFLOW

NOTES: M   T   W   T   F   S   S

THIS WEEK'S AFFIRMATION:

THIS WEEK'S HIGH POINT:

I'M GRATEFUL FOR:

THIS WEEK'S DISTRACTION:

HOW CAN I IMPROVE?

REMINDERS:

Priority

WEEKLY PLANNER

Eat the Frog

Week of: _____

WEEKLY FOCUS

Health & Wellness	Business	Craft

Monday
1 HOUR SPRINT

Fuel
Vitamins

Word count: ___K

Tuesday
1 HOUR SPRINT

Fuel
Vitamins

Word count: ___K

Wednesday
1 HOUR SPRINT

Fuel
Vitamins

Word count: ___K

Thursday
1 HOUR SPRINT

Fuel
Vitamins

Word count: ___K

Friday
1 HOUR SPRINT

Fuel
Vitamins

Word count: ___K

To-Do List

- ☐ _____
- ☐ _____
- ☐ _____
- ☐ _____
- ☐ _____
- ☐ _____
- ☐ _____

Email / 20 Min Social

- ☐ M M ☐
- ☐ T T ☐
- ☐ W W ☐
- ☐ T T ☐
- ☐ F F ☐

Random Acts of Kindness
☐ ☐ ☐

Weekend

Next Week

OVERFLOW

NOTES: M T W T F S S

THIS WEEK'S AFFIRMATION:

THIS WEEK'S HIGH POINT: | **I'M GRATEFUL FOR:**

THIS WEEK'S DISTRACTION: | **HOW CAN I IMPROVE?**

REMINDERS:

Priority

WEEKLY PLANNER

Eat the Frog

Week of: _____

WEEKLY FOCUS

Health & Wellness	Business	Craft

Monday
1 HOUR SPRINT

Fuel Vitamins

Word count: ___K

Tuesday
1 HOUR SPRINT

Fuel Vitamins

Word count: ___K

Wednesday
1 HOUR SPRINT

Fuel Vitamins

Word count: ___K

Thursday
1 HOUR SPRINT

Fuel Vitamins

Word count: ___K

Friday
1 HOUR SPRINT

Fuel Vitamins

Word count: ___K

To-Do List
☐ _____
☐ _____
☐ _____
☐ _____
☐ _____
☐ _____
☐ _____
☐ _____

Email   20 Min Social

☐ M   M ☐
☐ T   T ☐
☐ W   W ☐
☐ T   T ☐
☐ F   F ☐

Random Acts of Kindness
☐ ☐ ☐

Weekend

Next Week

OVERFLOW

NOTES: M T W T F S S

THIS WEEK'S AFFIRMATION:

THIS WEEK'S HIGH POINT:

I'M GRATEFUL FOR:

THIS WEEK'S DISTRACTION:

HOW CAN I IMPROVE?

REMINDERS:

WEEKLY PLANNER

Priority

Eat the Frog

Week of: _____

WEEKLY FOCUS

Health & Wellness	Business	Craft

Monday
1 HOUR SPRINT ☐

Fuel
Vitamins

Word count: ___K

Tuesday
1 HOUR SPRINT ☐

Fuel
Vitamins

Word count: ___K

Wednesday
1 HOUR SPRINT ☐

Fuel
Vitamins

Word count: ___K

Thursday
1 HOUR SPRINT ☐

Fuel
Vitamins

Word count: ___K

Friday
1 HOUR SPRINT ☐

Fuel
Vitamins

Word count: ___K

To-Do List
- ☐ _____
- ☐ _____
- ☐ _____
- ☐ _____
- ☐ _____
- ☐ _____
- ☐ _____
- ☐ _____

Email
- ☐ M
- ☐ T
- ☐ W
- ☐ T
- ☐ F

20 Min Social
- M ☐
- T ☐
- W ☐
- T ☐
- F ☐

Random Acts of Kindness
☐ ☐ ☐

Weekend

Next Week

OVERFLOW

NOTES: M T W T F S S

THIS WEEK'S AFFIRMATION:

THIS WEEK'S HIGH POINT:

I'M GRATEFUL FOR:

THIS WEEK'S DISTRACTION:

HOW CAN I IMPROVE?

REMINDERS:

Priority

WEEKLY PLANNER

Eat the Frog

Week of: _____

WEEKLY FOCUS

Health & Wellness | Business | Craft

Monday	Tuesday	Wednesday	Thursday	Friday
1 HOUR SPRINT	1 HOUR SPRINT	1 HOUR SPRINT	1 HOUR SPRINT	1 HOUR SPRINT

Fuel Vitamins (x5)

Word count: ___K

To-Do List | Email | 20 Min Social | Weekend | Next Week

☐ M M ☐
☐ T T ☐
☐ W W ☐
☐ T T ☐
☐ F F ☐

Random Acts of Kindness

☐ ☐ ☐

OVERFLOW

NOTES: M T W T F S S

THIS WEEK'S AFFIRMATION:

THIS WEEK'S HIGH POINT:

I'M GRATEFUL FOR:

THIS WEEK'S DISTRACTION:

HOW CAN I IMPROVE?

REMINDERS:

Priority

WEEKLY PLANNER

Eat the Frog

Week of: _____

WEEKLY FOCUS

Health & Wellness	Business	Craft

Monday
1 HOUR SPRINT

Fuel
Vitamins

Word count: ___K

Tuesday
1 HOUR SPRINT

Fuel
Vitamins

Word count: ___K

Wednesday
1 HOUR SPRINT

Fuel
Vitamins

Word count: ___K

Thursday
1 HOUR SPRINT

Fuel
Vitamins

Word count: ___K

Friday
1 HOUR SPRINT

Fuel
Vitamins

Word count: ___K

To-Do List

☐ _____
☐ _____
☐ _____
☐ _____
☐ _____
☐ _____
☐ _____

Email

☐ M
☐ T
☐ W
☐ T
☐ F

20 Min Social

M ☐
T ☐
W ☐
T ☐
F ☐

Weekend

Next Week

Random Acts of Kindness

☐ ☐ ☐

OVERFLOW

NOTES: M T W T F S S

THIS WEEK'S AFFIRMATION:

THIS WEEK'S HIGH POINT:

I'M GRATEFUL FOR:

THIS WEEK'S DISTRACTION:

HOW CAN I IMPROVE?

REMINDERS:

Priority

WEEKLY PLANNER

Eat the Frog

Week of: _____

WEEKLY FOCUS

Health & Wellness	Business	Craft

Monday
1 HOUR SPRINT

Fuel
Vitamins

Word count: ___K

Tuesday
1 HOUR SPRINT

Fuel
Vitamins

Word count: ___K

Wednesday
1 HOUR SPRINT

Fuel
Vitamins

Word count: ___K

Thursday
1 HOUR SPRINT

Fuel
Vitamins

Word count: ___K

Friday
1 HOUR SPRINT

Fuel
Vitamins

Word count: ___K

To-Do List

- ☐ _____
- ☐ _____
- ☐ _____
- ☐ _____
- ☐ _____
- ☐ _____
- ☐ _____

Email
☐ M
☐ T
☐ W
☐ T
☐ F

20 Min Social
M ☐
T ☐
W ☐
T ☐
F ☐

Random Acts of Kindness
☐ ☐ ☐

Weekend

Next Week

OVERFLOW

NOTES: M T W T F S S

THIS WEEK'S AFFIRMATION:

THIS WEEK'S HIGH POINT:

I'M GRATEFUL FOR:

THIS WEEK'S DISTRACTION:

HOW CAN I IMPROVE?

REMINDERS:

Priority

WEEKLY PLANNER

Eat the Frog

Week of: _____

WEEKLY FOCUS

Health & Wellness	Business	Craft

Monday
1 HOUR SPRINT

Fuel
Vitamins

Word count: ___K

Tuesday
1 HOUR SPRINT

Fuel
Vitamins

Word count: ___K

Wednesday
1 HOUR SPRINT

Fuel
Vitamins

Word count: ___K

Thursday
1 HOUR SPRINT

Fuel
Vitamins

Word count: ___K

Friday
1 HOUR SPRINT

Fuel
Vitamins

Word count: ___K

To-Do List
- ☐ _____
- ☐ _____
- ☐ _____
- ☐ _____
- ☐ _____
- ☐ _____
- ☐ _____
- ☐ _____

Email / 20 Min Social

☐ M   M ☐
☐ T   T ☐
☐ W   W ☐
☐ T   T ☐
☐ F   F ☐

Random Acts of Kindness
☐ ☐ ☐

Weekend

Next Week

OVERFLOW

NOTES: M T W T F S S

THIS WEEK'S AFFIRMATION:

THIS WEEK'S HIGH POINT:

I'M GRATEFUL FOR:

THIS WEEK'S DISTRACTION:

HOW CAN I IMPROVE?

REMINDERS:

Priority

WEEKLY PLANNER

Eat the Frog

Week of: _____

WEEKLY FOCUS

Health & Wellness	Business	Craft

Monday
1 HOUR SPRINT

Fuel
Vitamins

Word count: ___K

Tuesday
1 HOUR SPRINT

Fuel
Vitamins

Word count: ___K

Wednesday
1 HOUR SPRINT

Fuel
Vitamins

Word count: ___K

Thursday
1 HOUR SPRINT

Fuel
Vitamins

Word count: ___K

Friday
1 HOUR SPRINT

Fuel
Vitamins

Word count: ___K

To-Do List   Email   20 Min Social   Weekend   Next Week

☐ _____
☐ _____
☐ _____
☐ _____
☐ _____
☐ _____
☐ _____
☐ _____

☐ M   M ☐
☐ T   T ☐
☐ W   W ☐
☐ T   T ☐
☐ F   F ☐

Random Acts of Kindness

☐ ☐ ☐

OVERFLOW

NOTES:	M T W T F S S

THIS WEEK'S AFFIRMATION:

THIS WEEK'S HIGH POINT:

I'M GRATEFUL FOR:

THIS WEEK'S DISTRACTION:

HOW CAN I IMPROVE?

REMINDERS:

Priority

WEEKLY PLANNER

Eat the Frog

Week of: _____

WEEKLY FOCUS

Health & Wellness	Business	Craft

Monday	Tuesday	Wednesday	Thursday	Friday
1 HOUR SPRINT	1 HOUR SPRINT	1 HOUR SPRINT	1 HOUR SPRINT	1 HOUR SPRINT
Fuel / Vitamins	Fuel / Vitamins	Fuel / Vitamins	Fuel / Vitamins	Fuel / Vitamins
Word count:___K	Word count:___K	Word count:___K	Word count:___K	Word count:___K

To-Do List   Email   20 Min Social   Weekend   Next Week

☐ M M ☐
☐ T T ☐
☐ W W ☐
☐ T T ☐
☐ F F ☐

Random Acts of Kindness
☐ ☐ ☐

OVERFLOW

NOTES: M T W T F S S

THIS WEEK'S AFFIRMATION:

THIS WEEK'S HIGH POINT:

I'M GRATEFUL FOR:

THIS WEEK'S DISTRACTION:

HOW CAN I IMPROVE?

REMINDERS:

Priority

WEEKLY PLANNER

Eat the Frog

Week of: _____

WEEKLY FOCUS

Health & Wellness	Business	Craft

Monday
1 HOUR SPRINT

Fuel Vitamins

Word count:___K

Tuesday
1 HOUR SPRINT

Fuel Vitamins

Word count:___K

Wednesday
1 HOUR SPRINT

Fuel Vitamins

Word count:___K

Thursday
1 HOUR SPRINT

Fuel Vitamins

Word count:___K

Friday
1 HOUR SPRINT

Fuel Vitamins

Word count:___K

To-Do List

- [ ] _____
- [ ] _____
- [ ] _____
- [ ] _____
- [ ] _____
- [ ] _____
- [ ] _____

Email

20 Min Social

- [ ] M   M [ ]
- [ ] T   T [ ]
- [ ] W   W [ ]
- [ ] T   T [ ]
- [ ] F   F [ ]

Random Acts of Kindness

[ ] [ ] [ ]

Weekend

Next Week

OVERFLOW

NOTES: M T W T F S S

THIS WEEK'S AFFIRMATION:

THIS WEEK'S HIGH POINT:

I'M GRATEFUL FOR:

THIS WEEK'S DISTRACTION:

HOW CAN I IMPROVE?

REMINDERS:

Priority

WEEKLY PLANNER

Eat the Frog

Week of: _____

WEEKLY FOCUS

Health & Wellness	Business	Craft

Monday
1 HOUR SPRINT

Fuel
Vitamins

Word count:___K

Tuesday
1 HOUR SPRINT

Fuel
Vitamins

Word count:___K

Wednesday
1 HOUR SPRINT

Fuel
Vitamins

Word count:___K

Thursday
1 HOUR SPRINT

Fuel
Vitamins

Word count:___K

Friday
1 HOUR SPRINT

Fuel
Vitamins

Word count:___K

To-Do List
- ☐ _____
- ☐ _____
- ☐ _____
- ☐ _____
- ☐ _____
- ☐ _____
- ☐ _____
- ☐ _____

Email
☐ M
☐ T
☐ W
☐ T
☐ F

20 Min Social
M ☐
T ☐
W ☐
T ☐
F ☐

Random Acts of Kindness
☐ ☐ ☐

Weekend

Next Week

OVERFLOW

NOTES: M   T   W   T   F   S   S

THIS WEEK'S AFFIRMATION:

THIS WEEK'S HIGH POINT:

I'M GRATEFUL FOR:

THIS WEEK'S DISTRACTION:

HOW CAN I IMPROVE?

REMINDERS:

Priority | # WEEKLY PLANNER | Eat the Frog

Week of: _____

WEEKLY FOCUS

Health & Wellness	Business	Craft

Monday
1 HOUR SPRINT

Fuel Vitamins

Word count: ___K

Tuesday
1 HOUR SPRINT

Fuel Vitamins

Word count: ___K

Wednesday
1 HOUR SPRINT

Fuel Vitamins

Word count: ___K

Thursday
1 HOUR SPRINT

Fuel Vitamins

Word count: ___K

Friday
1 HOUR SPRINT

Fuel Vitamins

Word count: ___K

To-Do List

☐ _____
☐ _____
☐ _____
☐ _____
☐ _____
☐ _____
☐ _____
☐ _____

Email

☐ M
☐ T
☐ W
☐ T
☐ F

20 Min Social

M ☐
T ☐
W ☐
T ☐
F ☐

Weekend

Next Week

Random Acts of Kindness

☐ ☐ ☐

OVERFLOW

NOTES: M T W T F S S

THIS WEEK'S AFFIRMATION:

THIS WEEK'S HIGH POINT:

I'M GRATEFUL FOR:

THIS WEEK'S DISTRACTION:

HOW CAN I IMPROVE?

REMINDERS:

Priority

WEEKLY PLANNER

Eat the Frog

Week of: _____

WEEKLY FOCUS

Health & Wellness	Business	Craft

Monday
1 HOUR SPRINT

Fuel
Vitamins

Word count: ___K

Tuesday
1 HOUR SPRINT

Fuel
Vitamins

Word count: ___K

Wednesday
1 HOUR SPRINT

Fuel
Vitamins

Word count: ___K

Thursday
1 HOUR SPRINT

Fuel
Vitamins

Word count: ___K

Friday
1 HOUR SPRINT

Fuel
Vitamins

Word count: ___K

To-Do List
- ☐ _____
- ☐ _____
- ☐ _____
- ☐ _____
- ☐ _____
- ☐ _____
- ☐ _____
- ☐ _____

Email
- ☐ M
- ☐ T
- ☐ W
- ☐ T
- ☐ F

20 Min Social
- M ☐
- T ☐
- W ☐
- T ☐
- F ☐

Random Acts of Kindness
☐ ☐ ☐

Weekend

Next Week

OVERFLOW

NOTES: M   T   W   T   F   S   S

THIS WEEK'S AFFIRMATION:

THIS WEEK'S HIGH POINT:

I'M GRATEFUL FOR:

THIS WEEK'S DISTRACTION:

HOW CAN I IMPROVE?

REMINDERS:

Priority

WEEKLY PLANNER

Eat the Frog

Week of: _____

WEEKLY FOCUS

Health & Wellness	Business	Craft

Monday
1 HOUR SPRINT

Fuel Vitamins

Word count: ___K

Tuesday
1 HOUR SPRINT

Fuel Vitamins

Word count: ___K

Wednesday
1 HOUR SPRINT

Fuel Vitamins

Word count: ___K

Thursday
1 HOUR SPRINT

Fuel Vitamins

Word count: ___K

Friday
1 HOUR SPRINT

Fuel Vitamins

Word count: ___K

To-Do List
- ☐ _____
- ☐ _____
- ☐ _____
- ☐ _____
- ☐ _____
- ☐ _____
- ☐ _____
- ☐ _____

Email
☐ M
☐ T
☐ W
☐ T
☐ F

20 Min Social
M ☐
T ☐
W ☐
T ☐
F ☐

Weekend

Next Week

Random Acts of Kindness
☐ ☐ ☐

OVERFLOW

NOTES: M T W T F S S

THIS WEEK'S AFFIRMATION:

THIS WEEK'S HIGH POINT:	I'M GRATEFUL FOR:
THIS WEEK'S DISTRACTION:	HOW CAN I IMPROVE?

REMINDERS:

Priority

WEEKLY PLANNER

Eat the Frog

Week of: _____

WEEKLY FOCUS

Health & Wellness	Business	Craft

Monday
1 HOUR SPRINT ☐

Fuel
Vitamins ☐

Word count: ___K

Tuesday
1 HOUR SPRINT ☐

Fuel
Vitamins ☐

Word count: ___K

Wednesday
1 HOUR SPRINT ☐

Fuel
Vitamins ☐

Word count: ___K

Thursday
1 HOUR SPRINT ☐

Fuel
Vitamins ☐

Word count: ___K

Friday
1 HOUR SPRINT ☐

Fuel
Vitamins ☐

Word count: ___K

To-Do List
☐ _____
☐ _____
☐ _____
☐ _____
☐ _____
☐ _____
☐ _____

Email
☐ M
☐ T
☐ W
☐ T
☐ F

20 Min Social
M ☐
T ☐
W ☐
T ☐
F ☐

Weekend

Next Week

Random Acts of Kindness
☐ ☐ ☐

OVERFLOW

NOTES: M T W T F S S

THIS WEEK'S AFFIRMATION:

THIS WEEK'S HIGH POINT:

I'M GRATEFUL FOR:

THIS WEEK'S DISTRACTION:

HOW CAN I IMPROVE?

REMINDERS:

Priority | # WEEKLY PLANNER | Eat the Frog

Week of: _____

WEEKLY FOCUS

Health & Wellness	Business	Craft

Monday
1 HOUR SPRINT

Fuel
Vitamins

Word count: ___K

Tuesday
1 HOUR SPRINT

Fuel
Vitamins

Word count: ___K

Wednesday
1 HOUR SPRINT

Fuel
Vitamins

Word count: ___K

Thursday
1 HOUR SPRINT

Fuel
Vitamins

Word count: ___K

Friday
1 HOUR SPRINT

Fuel
Vitamins

Word count: ___K

To-Do List

☐ _____
☐ _____
☐ _____
☐ _____
☐ _____
☐ _____
☐ _____
☐ _____

Email | 20 Min Social

☐ M   M ☐
☐ T   T ☐
☐ W   W ☐
☐ T   T ☐
☐ F   F ☐

Random Acts of Kindness

☐ ☐ ☐

Weekend

Next Week

OVERFLOW

NOTES: M T W T F S S

THIS WEEK'S AFFIRMATION:

THIS WEEK'S HIGH POINT:

I'M GRATEFUL FOR:

THIS WEEK'S DISTRACTION:

HOW CAN I IMPROVE?

REMINDERS:

Priority | Eat the Frog

WEEKLY PLANNER

Week of: _____

WEEKLY FOCUS

Health & Wellness	Business	Craft

Monday
1 HOUR SPRINT

Fuel / Vitamins

Word count: ___K

Tuesday
1 HOUR SPRINT

Fuel / Vitamins

Word count: ___K

Wednesday
1 HOUR SPRINT

Fuel / Vitamins

Word count: ___K

Thursday
1 HOUR SPRINT

Fuel / Vitamins

Word count: ___K

Friday
1 HOUR SPRINT

Fuel / Vitamins

Word count: ___K

To-Do List

- ☐ _____
- ☐ _____
- ☐ _____
- ☐ _____
- ☐ _____
- ☐ _____
- ☐ _____
- ☐ _____

Email

- ☐ M
- ☐ T
- ☐ W
- ☐ T
- ☐ F

20 Min Social

- M ☐
- T ☐
- W ☐
- T ☐
- F ☐

Random Acts of Kindness

☐ ☐ ☐

Weekend

Next Week

OVERFLOW

NOTES: M T W T F S S

THIS WEEK'S AFFIRMATION:

THIS WEEK'S HIGH POINT:

I'M GRATEFUL FOR:

THIS WEEK'S DISTRACTION:

HOW CAN I IMPROVE?

REMINDERS:

Priority

WEEKLY PLANNER

Eat the Frog

Week of: _____

WEEKLY FOCUS

Health & Wellness	Business	Craft

Monday
1 HOUR SPRINT

Fuel
Vitamins

Word count: ___K

Tuesday
1 HOUR SPRINT

Fuel
Vitamins

Word count: ___K

Wednesday
1 HOUR SPRINT

Fuel
Vitamins

Word count: ___K

Thursday
1 HOUR SPRINT

Fuel
Vitamins

Word count: ___K

Friday
1 HOUR SPRINT

Fuel
Vitamins

Word count: ___K

To-Do List
- ☐ _____
- ☐ _____
- ☐ _____
- ☐ _____
- ☐ _____
- ☐ _____
- ☐ _____
- ☐ _____

Email
☐ M
☐ T
☐ W
☐ T
☐ F

20 Min Social
M ☐
T ☐
W ☐
T ☐
F ☐

Random Acts of Kindness
☐ ☐ ☐

Weekend

Next Week

OVERFLOW

NOTES:　　　　　　　　　　　M T W T F S S

THIS WEEK'S AFFIRMATION:

THIS WEEK'S HIGH POINT:

I'M GRATEFUL FOR:

THIS WEEK'S DISTRACTION:

HOW CAN I IMPROVE?

REMINDERS:

Priority

WEEKLY PLANNER

Eat the Frog

Week of: _____

WEEKLY FOCUS

Health & Wellness	Business	Craft

Monday
1 HOUR SPRINT

Fuel
Vitamins

Word count: ___K

Tuesday
1 HOUR SPRINT

Fuel
Vitamins

Word count: ___K

Wednesday
1 HOUR SPRINT

Fuel
Vitamins

Word count: ___K

Thursday
1 HOUR SPRINT

Fuel
Vitamins

Word count: ___K

Friday
1 HOUR SPRINT

Fuel
Vitamins

Word count: ___K

To-Do List

☐ _____
☐ _____
☐ _____
☐ _____
☐ _____
☐ _____
☐ _____
☐ _____

Email

☐ M
☐ T
☐ W
☐ T
☐ F

20 Min Social

M ☐
T ☐
W ☐
T ☐
F ☐

Random Acts of Kindness

☐ ☐ ☐

Weekend

Next Week

OVERFLOW

NOTES: M T W T F S S

THIS WEEK'S AFFIRMATION:

THIS WEEK'S HIGH POINT:

I'M GRATEFUL FOR:

THIS WEEK'S DISTRACTION:

HOW CAN I IMPROVE?

REMINDERS:

Priority

WEEKLY PLANNER

Eat the Frog

Week of: _____

WEEKLY FOCUS

Health & Wellness	Business	Craft

Monday
1 HOUR SPRINT

Fuel Vitamins

Word count: ___K

Tuesday
1 HOUR SPRINT

Fuel Vitamins

Word count: ___K

Wednesday
1 HOUR SPRINT

Fuel Vitamins

Word count: ___K

Thursday
1 HOUR SPRINT

Fuel Vitamins

Word count: ___K

Friday
1 HOUR SPRINT

Fuel Vitamins

Word count: ___K

To-Do List
- ☐ _____
- ☐ _____
- ☐ _____
- ☐ _____
- ☐ _____
- ☐ _____
- ☐ _____
- ☐ _____

Email
- ☐ M
- ☐ T
- ☐ W
- ☐ T
- ☐ F

20 Min Social
- M ☐
- T ☐
- W ☐
- T ☐
- F ☐

Random Acts of Kindness
☐ ☐ ☐

Weekend

Next Week

OVERFLOW

NOTES: M T W T F S S

THIS WEEK'S AFFIRMATION:

THIS WEEK'S HIGH POINT:

I'M GRATEFUL FOR:

THIS WEEK'S DISTRACTION:

HOW CAN I IMPROVE?

REMINDERS:

Priority

WEEKLY PLANNER

Eat the Frog

Week of: _____

WEEKLY FOCUS

Health & Wellness	Business	Craft

Monday	Tuesday	Wednesday	Thursday	Friday
1 HOUR SPRINT	1 HOUR SPRINT	1 HOUR SPRINT	1 HOUR SPRINT	1 HOUR SPRINT
Fuel / Vitamins	Fuel / Vitamins	Fuel / Vitamins	Fuel / Vitamins	Fuel / Vitamins
Word count: ___K	Word count: ___K	Word count: ___K	Word count: ___K	Word count: ___K

To-Do List

☐ _____
☐ _____
☐ _____
☐ _____
☐ _____
☐ _____
☐ _____
☐ _____

Email   20 Min Social

☐ M   M ☐
☐ T   T ☐
☐ W   W ☐
☐ T   T ☐
☐ F   F ☐

Random Acts of Kindness

☐ ☐ ☐

Weekend

Next Week

OVERFLOW

NOTES: M T W T F S S

THIS WEEK'S AFFIRMATION:

THIS WEEK'S HIGH POINT:

I'M GRATEFUL FOR:

THIS WEEK'S DISTRACTION:

HOW CAN I IMPROVE?

REMINDERS:

Priority

WEEKLY PLANNER

Eat the Frog

Week of: _____

WEEKLY FOCUS

Health & Wellness	Business	Craft

Monday
1 HOUR SPRINT

Fuel
Vitamins

Word count:___K

Tuesday
1 HOUR SPRINT

Fuel
Vitamins

Word count:___K

Wednesday
1 HOUR SPRINT

Fuel
Vitamins

Word count:___K

Thursday
1 HOUR SPRINT

Fuel
Vitamins

Word count:___K

Friday
1 HOUR SPRINT

Fuel
Vitamins

Word count:___K

To-Do List
- ☐ _____
- ☐ _____
- ☐ _____
- ☐ _____
- ☐ _____
- ☐ _____
- ☐ _____
- ☐ _____

Email
☐ M
☐ T
☐ W
☐ T
☐ F

20 Min Social
M ☐
T ☐
W ☐
T ☐
F ☐

Random Acts of Kindness
☐ ☐ ☐

Weekend

Next Week

OVERFLOW

NOTES: M T W T F S S

THIS WEEK'S AFFIRMATION:

THIS WEEK'S HIGH POINT:

I'M GRATEFUL FOR:

THIS WEEK'S DISTRACTION:

HOW CAN I IMPROVE?

REMINDERS:

Priority

WEEKLY PLANNER

Eat the Frog

Week of: _____

WEEKLY FOCUS

Health & Wellness	Business	Craft

Monday
1 HOUR SPRINT

Fuel Vitamins

Word count: ___K

Tuesday
1 HOUR SPRINT

Fuel Vitamins

Word count: ___K

Wednesday
1 HOUR SPRINT

Fuel Vitamins

Word count: ___K

Thursday
1 HOUR SPRINT

Fuel Vitamins

Word count: ___K

Friday
1 HOUR SPRINT

Fuel Vitamins

Word count: ___K

To-Do List

☐ _____
☐ _____
☐ _____
☐ _____
☐ _____
☐ _____
☐ _____
☐ _____

Email

20 Min Social

☐ M   M ☐
☐ T   T ☐
☐ W   W ☐
☐ T   T ☐
☐ F   F ☐

Random Acts of Kindness

☐ ☐ ☐

Weekend

Next Week

OVERFLOW

NOTES: M   T   W   T   F   S   S

THIS WEEK'S AFFIRMATION:

THIS WEEK'S HIGH POINT:

I'M GRATEFUL FOR:

THIS WEEK'S DISTRACTION:

HOW CAN I IMPROVE?

REMINDERS:

Priority

WEEKLY PLANNER

Eat the Frog

Week of: _____

WEEKLY FOCUS

Health & Wellness	Business	Craft

Monday
1 HOUR SPRINT

Fuel Vitamins

Word count: ___K

Tuesday
1 HOUR SPRINT

Fuel Vitamins

Word count: ___K

Wednesday
1 HOUR SPRINT

Fuel Vitamins

Word count: ___K

Thursday
1 HOUR SPRINT

Fuel Vitamins

Word count: ___K

Friday
1 HOUR SPRINT

Fuel Vitamins

Word count: ___K

To-Do List
☐ _____
☐ _____
☐ _____
☐ _____
☐ _____
☐ _____
☐ _____
☐ _____

Email / 20 Min Social
☐ M   M ☐
☐ T   T ☐
☐ W   W ☐
☐ T   T ☐
☐ F   F ☐

Random Acts of Kindness
☐ ☐ ☐

Weekend

Next Week

OVERFLOW

NOTES: M T W T F S S

THIS WEEK'S AFFIRMATION:

THIS WEEK'S HIGH POINT:

I'M GRATEFUL FOR:

THIS WEEK'S DISTRACTION:

HOW CAN I IMPROVE?

REMINDERS:

Priority

WEEKLY PLANNER

Eat the Frog

Week of: _____

WEEKLY FOCUS

Health & Wellness	Business	Craft

Monday
1 HOUR SPRINT

Fuel
Vitamins

Word count: ___K

Tuesday
1 HOUR SPRINT

Fuel
Vitamins

Word count: ___K

Wednesday
1 HOUR SPRINT

Fuel
Vitamins

Word count: ___K

Thursday
1 HOUR SPRINT

Fuel
Vitamins

Word count: ___K

Friday
1 HOUR SPRINT

Fuel
Vitamins

Word count: ___K

To-Do List
- [ ] _____
- [ ] _____
- [ ] _____
- [ ] _____
- [ ] _____
- [ ] _____
- [ ] _____
- [ ] _____

Email
- [ ] M
- [ ] T
- [ ] W
- [ ] T
- [ ] F

20 Min Social
- [ ] M
- [ ] T
- [ ] W
- [ ] T
- [ ] F

Weekend

Next Week

Random Acts of Kindness
- [ ] [ ] [ ]

OVERFLOW

NOTES: M T W T F S S

THIS WEEK'S AFFIRMATION:

THIS WEEK'S HIGH POINT:

I'M GRATEFUL FOR:

THIS WEEK'S DISTRACTION:

HOW CAN I IMPROVE?

REMINDERS:

Priority

WEEKLY PLANNER

Eat the Frog

Week of: _____

WEEKLY FOCUS

Health & Wellness	Business	Craft

Monday	Tuesday	Wednesday	Thursday	Friday
1 HOUR SPRINT	1 HOUR SPRINT	1 HOUR SPRINT	1 HOUR SPRINT	1 HOUR SPRINT

Fuel Vitamins (x5)

Word count: ___K

To-Do List

Email   20 Min Social

☐ M   M ☐
☐ T   T ☐
☐ W   W ☐
☐ T   T ☐
☐ F   F ☐

Weekend

Next Week

Random Acts of Kindness
☐ ☐ ☐

OVERFLOW

NOTES: M T W T F S S

THIS WEEK'S AFFIRMATION:

THIS WEEK'S HIGH POINT:

I'M GRATEFUL FOR:

THIS WEEK'S DISTRACTION:

HOW CAN I IMPROVE?

REMINDERS:

Priority | # WEEKLY PLANNER | Eat the Frog

Week of: _____

WEEKLY FOCUS

Health & Wellness	Business	Craft

Monday	Tuesday	Wednesday	Thursday	Friday
1 HOUR SPRINT	1 HOUR SPRINT	1 HOUR SPRINT	1 HOUR SPRINT	1 HOUR SPRINT
Fuel / Vitamins	Fuel / Vitamins	Fuel / Vitamins	Fuel / Vitamins	Fuel / Vitamins
Word count: ___K	Word count: ___K	Word count: ___K	Word count: ___K	Word count: ___K

To-Do List
- ☐ _____
- ☐ _____
- ☐ _____
- ☐ _____
- ☐ _____
- ☐ _____
- ☐ _____

Email | 20 Min Social

☐ M   M ☐
☐ T   T ☐
☐ W   W ☐
☐ T   T ☐
☐ F   F ☐

Random Acts of Kindness
☐ ☐ ☐

Weekend

Next Week

OVERFLOW

NOTES: M   T   W   T   F   S   S

THIS WEEK'S AFFIRMATION:

THIS WEEK'S HIGH POINT:

I'M GRATEFUL FOR:

THIS WEEK'S DISTRACTION:

HOW CAN I IMPROVE?

REMINDERS:

Priority

WEEKLY PLANNER

Eat the Frog

Week of: _____

WEEKLY FOCUS

Health & Wellness	Business	Craft

Monday
1 HOUR SPRINT

Fuel
Vitamins

Word count: ___K

Tuesday
1 HOUR SPRINT

Fuel
Vitamins

Word count: ___K

Wednesday
1 HOUR SPRINT

Fuel
Vitamins

Word count: ___K

Thursday
1 HOUR SPRINT

Fuel
Vitamins

Word count: ___K

Friday
1 HOUR SPRINT

Fuel
Vitamins

Word count: ___K

To-Do List
- ☐ _____
- ☐ _____
- ☐ _____
- ☐ _____
- ☐ _____
- ☐ _____
- ☐ _____
- ☐ _____

Email
- ☐ M
- ☐ T
- ☐ W
- ☐ T
- ☐ F

20 Min Social
- M ☐
- T ☐
- W ☐
- T ☐
- F ☐

Random Acts of Kindness
☐ ☐ ☐

Weekend

Next Week

OVERFLOW

NOTES: M T W T F S S

THIS WEEK'S AFFIRMATION:

THIS WEEK'S HIGH POINT:

I'M GRATEFUL FOR:

THIS WEEK'S DISTRACTION:

HOW CAN I IMPROVE?

REMINDERS:

Priority

WEEKLY PLANNER

Eat the Frog

Week of: _____

WEEKLY FOCUS

Health & Wellness	Business	Craft

Monday
1 HOUR SPRINT

Fuel
Vitamins

Word count: ___K

Tuesday
1 HOUR SPRINT

Fuel
Vitamins

Word count: ___K

Wednesday
1 HOUR SPRINT

Fuel
Vitamins

Word count: ___K

Thursday
1 HOUR SPRINT

Fuel
Vitamins

Word count: ___K

Friday
1 HOUR SPRINT

Fuel
Vitamins

Word count: ___K

To-Do List
- ☐ _____
- ☐ _____
- ☐ _____
- ☐ _____
- ☐ _____
- ☐ _____
- ☐ _____
- ☐ _____

Email
- ☐ M
- ☐ T
- ☐ W
- ☐ T
- ☐ F

20 Min Social
- M ☐
- T ☐
- W ☐
- T ☐
- F ☐

Random Acts of Kindness
☐ ☐ ☐

Weekend

Next Week

OVERFLOW

NOTES: M   T   W   T   F   S   S

THIS WEEK'S AFFIRMATION:

THIS WEEK'S HIGH POINT:

I'M GRATEFUL FOR:

THIS WEEK'S DISTRACTION:

HOW CAN I IMPROVE?

REMINDERS:

Priority

WEEKLY PLANNER

Eat the Frog

Week of: _____

WEEKLY FOCUS

Health & Wellness	Business	Craft

Monday
1 HOUR SPRINT

Fuel Vitamins

Word count: ___K

Tuesday
1 HOUR SPRINT

Fuel Vitamins

Word count: ___K

Wednesday
1 HOUR SPRINT

Fuel Vitamins

Word count: ___K

Thursday
1 HOUR SPRINT

Fuel Vitamins

Word count: ___K

Friday
1 HOUR SPRINT

Fuel Vitamins

Word count: ___K

To-Do List
- ☐ _____
- ☐ _____
- ☐ _____
- ☐ _____
- ☐ _____
- ☐ _____
- ☐ _____
- ☐ _____

Email
- ☐ M
- ☐ T
- ☐ W
- ☐ T
- ☐ F

20 Min Social
- M ☐
- T ☐
- W ☐
- T ☐
- F ☐

Random Acts of Kindness
☐ ☐ ☐

Weekend

Next Week

OVERFLOW

NOTES: M T W T F S S

THIS WEEK'S AFFIRMATION:

THIS WEEK'S HIGH POINT:

I'M GRATEFUL FOR:

THIS WEEK'S DISTRACTION:

HOW CAN I IMPROVE?

REMINDERS:

Priority

WEEKLY PLANNER

Eat the Frog

Week of: _____

WEEKLY FOCUS

Health & Wellness	Business	Craft

Monday
1 HOUR SPRINT

Fuel | Vitamins

Word count: ___K

Tuesday
1 HOUR SPRINT

Fuel | Vitamins

Word count: ___K

Wednesday
1 HOUR SPRINT

Fuel | Vitamins

Word count: ___K

Thursday
1 HOUR SPRINT

Fuel | Vitamins

Word count: ___K

Friday
1 HOUR SPRINT

Fuel | Vitamins

Word count: ___K

To-Do List
- ☐ _____
- ☐ _____
- ☐ _____
- ☐ _____
- ☐ _____
- ☐ _____
- ☐ _____
- ☐ _____

Email
- ☐ M
- ☐ T
- ☐ W
- ☐ T
- ☐ F

20 Min Social
- M ☐
- T ☐
- W ☐
- T ☐
- F ☐

Random Acts of Kindness
☐ ☐ ☐

Weekend

Next Week

OVERFLOW

NOTES: M T W T F S S

THIS WEEK'S AFFIRMATION:

THIS WEEK'S HIGH POINT:

I'M GRATEFUL FOR:

THIS WEEK'S DISTRACTION:

HOW CAN I IMPROVE?

REMINDERS:

Priority

WEEKLY PLANNER

Eat the Frog

Week of: _____

WEEKLY FOCUS

Health & Wellness	Business	Craft

Monday	Tuesday	Wednesday	Thursday	Friday
1 HOUR SPRINT	1 HOUR SPRINT	1 HOUR SPRINT	1 HOUR SPRINT	1 HOUR SPRINT
Fuel / Vitamins	Fuel / Vitamins	Fuel / Vitamins	Fuel / Vitamins	Fuel / Vitamins
Word count:___K	Word count:___K	Word count:___K	Word count:___K	Word count:___K

To-Do List

- ☐ _____
- ☐ _____
- ☐ _____
- ☐ _____
- ☐ _____
- ☐ _____
- ☐ _____
- ☐ _____

Email

☐ M   M ☐
☐ T   T ☐
☐ W   W ☐
☐ T   T ☐
☐ F   F ☐

20 Min Social

Random Acts of Kindness

☐ ☐ ☐

Weekend

Next Week

OVERFLOW

NOTES: M T W T F S S

THIS WEEK'S AFFIRMATION:

THIS WEEK'S HIGH POINT:

I'M GRATEFUL FOR:

THIS WEEK'S DISTRACTION:

HOW CAN I IMPROVE?

REMINDERS:

Priority

WEEKLY PLANNER

Eat the Frog

Week of: _____

WEEKLY FOCUS

Health & Wellness	Business	Craft

Monday	Tuesday	Wednesday	Thursday	Friday
1 HOUR SPRINT	1 HOUR SPRINT	1 HOUR SPRINT	1 HOUR SPRINT	1 HOUR SPRINT
Fuel / Vitamins	Fuel / Vitamins	Fuel / Vitamins	Fuel / Vitamins	Fuel / Vitamins
Word count:___K	Word count:___K	Word count:___K	Word count:___K	Word count:___K

To-Do List   Email   20 Min Social   Weekend   Next Week

- ☐ _____
- ☐ _____
- ☐ _____
- ☐ _____
- ☐ _____
- ☐ _____
- ☐ _____
- ☐ _____

☐ M   M ☐
☐ T   T ☐
☐ W   W ☐
☐ T   T ☐
☐ F   F ☐

Random Acts of Kindness

☐ ☐ ☐

OVERFLOW

NOTES: M   T   W   T   F   S   S

THIS WEEK'S AFFIRMATION:

THIS WEEK'S HIGH POINT:

I'M GRATEFUL FOR:

THIS WEEK'S DISTRACTION:

HOW CAN I IMPROVE?

REMINDERS:

Priority | # WEEKLY PLANNER | Eat the Frog

Week of: _____

WEEKLY FOCUS

Health & Wellness	Business	Craft

Monday
1 HOUR SPRINT

Fuel
Vitamins

Word count: ___K

Tuesday
1 HOUR SPRINT

Fuel
Vitamins

Word count: ___K

Wednesday
1 HOUR SPRINT

Fuel
Vitamins

Word count: ___K

Thursday
1 HOUR SPRINT

Fuel
Vitamins

Word count: ___K

Friday
1 HOUR SPRINT

Fuel
Vitamins

Word count: ___K

To-Do List
☐ _____
☐ _____
☐ _____
☐ _____
☐ _____
☐ _____
☐ _____
☐ _____

Email
☐ M
☐ T
☐ W
☐ T
☐ F

20 Min Social
M ☐
T ☐
W ☐
T ☐
F ☐

Random Acts of Kindness
☐ ☐ ☐

Weekend

Next Week

OVERFLOW

NOTES: M T W T F S S

THIS WEEK'S AFFIRMATION:

THIS WEEK'S HIGH POINT:

I'M GRATEFUL FOR:

THIS WEEK'S DISTRACTION:

HOW CAN I IMPROVE?

REMINDERS:

Priority

WEEKLY PLANNER

Eat the Frog

Week of: _____

WEEKLY FOCUS

Health & Wellness	Business	Craft

Monday
1 HOUR SPRINT

Fuel Vitamins

Word count: ___K

Tuesday
1 HOUR SPRINT

Fuel Vitamins

Word count: ___K

Wednesday
1 HOUR SPRINT

Fuel Vitamins

Word count: ___K

Thursday
1 HOUR SPRINT

Fuel Vitamins

Word count: ___K

Friday
1 HOUR SPRINT

Fuel Vitamins

Word count: ___K

To-Do List
- ☐ _____
- ☐ _____
- ☐ _____
- ☐ _____
- ☐ _____
- ☐ _____
- ☐ _____
- ☐ _____

Email
- ☐ M
- ☐ T
- ☐ W
- ☐ T
- ☐ F

20 Min Social
- M ☐
- T ☐
- W ☐
- T ☐
- F ☐

Random Acts of Kindness
☐ ☐ ☐

Weekend

Next Week

OVERFLOW

NOTES: M T W T F S S

THIS WEEK'S AFFIRMATION:

THIS WEEK'S HIGH POINT:

I'M GRATEFUL FOR:

THIS WEEK'S DISTRACTION:

HOW CAN I IMPROVE?

REMINDERS:

Priority

WEEKLY PLANNER

Eat the Frog

Week of: _____

WEEKLY FOCUS

Health & Wellness	Business	Craft

Monday
1 HOUR SPRINT

Fuel
Vitamins

Word count:___K

Tuesday
1 HOUR SPRINT

Fuel
Vitamins

Word count:___K

Wednesday
1 HOUR SPRINT

Fuel
Vitamins

Word count:___K

Thursday
1 HOUR SPRINT

Fuel
Vitamins

Word count:___K

Friday
1 HOUR SPRINT

Fuel
Vitamins

Word count:___K

To-Do List

☐ _____
☐ _____
☐ _____
☐ _____
☐ _____
☐ _____
☐ _____
☐ _____

Email

☐ M
☐ T
☐ W
☐ T
☐ F

20 Min Social

M ☐
T ☐
W ☐
T ☐
F ☐

Random Acts of Kindness

☐ ☐ ☐

Weekend

Next Week

OVERFLOW

NOTES: M T W T F S S

THIS WEEK'S AFFIRMATION:

THIS WEEK'S HIGH POINT:

I'M GRATEFUL FOR:

THIS WEEK'S DISTRACTION:

HOW CAN I IMPROVE?

REMINDERS:

Priority

WEEKLY PLANNER

Eat the Frog

Week of: _____

WEEKLY FOCUS

Health & Wellness	Business	Craft

Monday
1 HOUR SPRINT

Fuel
Vitamins

Word count:___K

Tuesday
1 HOUR SPRINT

Fuel
Vitamins

Word count:___K

Wednesday
1 HOUR SPRINT

Fuel
Vitamins

Word count:___K

Thursday
1 HOUR SPRINT

Fuel
Vitamins

Word count:___K

Friday
1 HOUR SPRINT

Fuel
Vitamins

Word count:___K

To-Do List
☐ _____
☐ _____
☐ _____
☐ _____
☐ _____
☐ _____
☐ _____
☐ _____

Email
☐ M
☐ T
☐ W
☐ T
☐ F

20 Min Social
M ☐
T ☐
W ☐
T ☐
F ☐

Random Acts of Kindness
☐ ☐ ☐

Weekend

Next Week

PART IV

RESOURCES

GENERAL PUNCTUATION RULES

When writing **dialogue**, all punctuation should go within the **quotation marks**.

Do not use **double punctuation** (?? or ?! or !!)

Do not use **parentheses** in fiction.

Avoid overused **exclamation points**. Only use when someone is screaming, angry, or especially excited. A raised voice does not warrant an exclamation point. They are rarely used in well-written fiction.

Colons are to be avoided and replaced with periods or em dashes in fiction.

Semicolons are to be avoided and replaced with periods or commas in fiction.

Em dashes indicate an interruption in speech or thought.

Ellipses indicate halting speech, a broken thought, or the trailing off of words. (I thought...)

Commas should be used:
- Before a dialogue tag ("Let's go," he said)
- To separate words, clauses, and phrases in a series (bananas, lemons, and plums)
- Before and after the name of a person being addressed (Hi, Jill, how are you?)
- For general pacing in a narrative to form a pause

Do not use commas for:
- Splices when two sentences would work (SPLICE: I don't want popcorn, I want candy. BETTER: I don't want popcorn. I want candy.)
- Action tags ("You've got to be kidding!" He laughed.)

CAPITALIZATION RULES

ALWAYS CAPITALIZE

- Book Titles
- Clubs
- Common nouns ONLY when functioning as names (Mom, Dad, Grammy)
- Days of the Week
- Directions with proper nouns (North Jersey)
- Eras
- Formal God references (God, Lord, Maker)
- Heaven, Hell, and Earth (when implying a place)
- Historic Events
- Holidays
- Months
- Organizations
- Publications
- Proper Nouns
- Song Titles
- Title preceding a proper noun (President Clinton)
- Trademarks (Monopoly)

NEVER CAPITALIZE

- Animals (tiger, gorilla)
- Career titles (lawyer, doctor)
- Dances (tango, waltz)
- Directions (north, south, east, west)
- Games (checkers)
- Generic god references (a sea god)
- Musical Instruments
- Plants
- Relationship nouns preceded by pronouns (<u>my</u> mom)
- Respectful references (yes, sir)
- School subjects
- Seasons
- Terms of endearment (babe, honey)

FORMATTING NUMBERS

SPELL IN WORDS

- Age
- Fractions
- Height
- Money
- Temperature
- Time
- Weight
- Whole Numbers
- Years

WRITE IN DIGITS

- Acts
- Addresses
- Dates
- Decades (1960's)
- Forms of Measurement
- Percentages (spell the word "*percent*")
- Whole Numbers and Fractions (3 1/8)
- Years (2021)

EXCEPTIONS TO THE RULE:

If a character is looking directly at a clock or sign and reading the numbers, the digital format would be used.

(Example: She glanced at her phone and the numbers glared 3:56.)

FILLER WORDS

about	his	the
all	in	then
and	into	they
as	it	to
but	just	up
by	little	very
down	of	was
for	out	well
from	really	were
had	she	which
he	so	while
her	that	

STALL PHRASES TO AVOID

attempted to	started to
seemed to	wanted to
tried to	reached for
going to	thinking about

OVERUSED WORDS

a bit	get	seen
a little	got	simply
a lot	had	slightly
about	half	small
actually	has	so
all	have	somehow
almost	here	something
already	highly	sometime
always	in	somewhat
and	into	sort of
appear	just	start
approximately	kind of	such
as	knew	suddenly
basically	knowing	that
because	large	than
been	like	then
began	momentarily	there
begin	mostly	therefore
begun	must	thing
being	names	to
caused	nearly	to be
close to	notice	truly
completely	now	unbeknownst
could	only	utterly
essentially	out	very
even	practically	was
eventually	pretty	watch
exactly	quite	were
extremely	rather	where
fairly	really	within
finally	seem(s)	would

DIALOGUE TAGS

accused
acknowledged
admitted
agreed
answered
argued
asked
barked
begged
bellowed
blustered
bragged
called
complained
confessed
cried
demanded
denied
growled
hinted
hissed
howled
inquired
interrupted
lied
mumbled
murmured
muttered

nagged
pleaded
promised
purred
questioned
replied
requested
retorted
roared
said
sang
screamed
screeched
shouted
snarled
sobbed
threatened
told
wailed
warned
whimpered
whined
whispered
yelled

ABOUT THE AUTHOR

Lydia Michaels is the author of over forty novels and the consecutive winner of the *2018 & 2019 Author of the Year Award* from *Happenings Media*, as well as the recipient of the *2014 Best Author Award* from the *Courier Times*. She has been featured in *USA Today*, *Romantic Times Magazine*, *Love & Lace*, and more. As the host and founder of the *East Coast Author Convention*, the *Behind the Keys Author Retreat*, and *Read Between the Wines*, she continues to celebrate her growing love for readers and romance novels around the world.

Lydia is happily married to her childhood sweetheart. Some of her favorite things include the scent of paperback books, listening to her husband play piano, escaping to her coastal home at the Jersey Shore, cheap wine, 80's pop culture, coffee, and kilts. She hopes to meet you soon at one of her many upcoming events.

Please follow and/or reach out to Lydia Michaels through email or social media. She is most interactive with bloggers, authors, and fans on the following platforms:

Email:
Lydia@LydiaMichaelsBooks.com

Instagram:
@Lydia_michaels_books
www.instagram.com/lydia_michaels_books

Facebook:
www.Facebook.com/LydiaMichaels

TikTok:
@lydiamichaels
www.tiktok.com/@lydiamichaels

LOOKING FOR MORE

The **Write 10K in a Day Author Planner** is part of the *Write 10K in a Day* series which includes Lydia Michaels' groundbreaking author guide, **Write 10K in a Day: Avoid Burnout and Unleash Your Prolific Potential** (available in print, digital, and **audiobook**), and the **Write 10K in a Day Workbook**.

The *Write 10K in a Day* text takes a comprehensive look at business essentials such as the publishing process, managing social media, finding a healthy balance between life and time on the job, and achieving sustainable success in the book industry. Michaels shares years of experience in a warm and personal manner that grips the reader, inspires, and even gets a few laughs.

For educational videos, author resources, and ongoing inspiration, follow Lydia Michaels and the *Write 10K in a Day* series on Instagram **@Write10KinaDay** and **@Lydia_Michaels_Books**.

Do you have suggestions to improve this planner or other books in the Write 10K in a Day series?

Email Lydia Michaels at Lydia@LydiaMichaelsBooks.com.

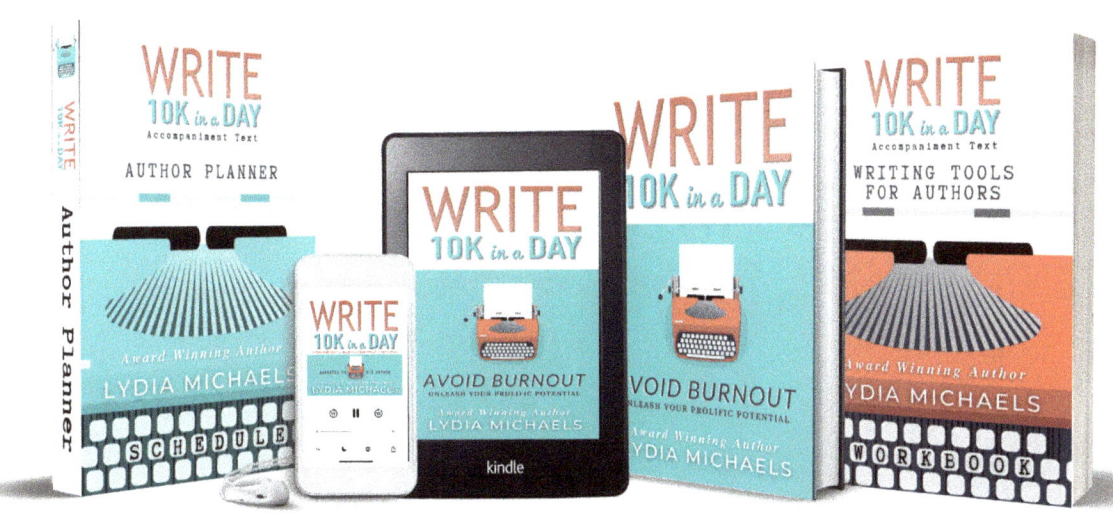

BOOKS BY LYDIA MICHAELS

Write 10K in a Day: Avoid Burnout Unleash Your Prolific Potential
Write 10K in a Day Workbook
Write 10K in a Day Author Planner
Wake My Heart
The Best Man
Love Me Nots
Pining For You
Original Sin
Dark Exodus
Sugar
Hurt
Calamity Rayne: Gets a Life
Calamity Rayne: Back Again
Forfeit
Lost Together
Atonement
Almost Priest
Beautiful Distraction
Irish Rogue
British Professor
Broken Man
Controlled Chaos
Intentional Risk
Hard Fix
First Comes Love
If I Fall
Something Borrowed
Falling In
Breaking Out
Coming Home
Sacrifice of the Pawn
Queen of the Knight
Breaking Perfect
Protege
Blind
Untied
La Vie en Rose
Simple Man
Remember Me

NOTES

NOTES

NOTES

www.ingramcontent.com/pod-product-compliance
Lightning Source LLC
Chambersburg PA
CBHW051119110526
44589CB00026B/2979